EVERYDAY TAO

Other books by Deng Ming-Dao

365 Tao: Daily Meditations

Chronicles of Tao: The Secret Life of a Taoist Master

Scholar Warrior: An Introduction to the Tao in Everyday Life

Everyday Tao

Living with Balance and Harmony

Deng Ming-Dao

Calligraphy by Edward E. Thi

HarperSanFrancisco
An Imprint of HarperCollinsPublishers

Acknowledgments

My thanks to Lillian and Phil Robyn for their friendship and support, and for their introduction to Professor Edward Thi.

Professor Thi provided patient explanations on many more obscure points of Chinese etymology, and also agreed to provide the elegant calligraphy shown throughout the book.

John Loudon and Ann Moru provided thoughtful and learned editing. Karen Levine, Terri Leonard, and Ralph Fowler shepherded this book through the intricacies of production.

My thanks, as always, to Betty, who maintains so much in our life together, and who makes time available for me to write.

HarperSanFrancisco and the author, in association with The Basic Foundation, a not-for-profit organization whose primary mission is reforestation, will facilitate the planting of two trees for every one tree used in the manufacture of this book.

A TREE CLAUSE BOOK

HarperCollins Web Site: http://www.harpercollins.com
HarperCollins®, 🖤 ®, HarperSanFrancisco™, and A TREE CLAUSE BOOK®
are trademarks of HarperCollins Publishers Inc.

FIRST EDITION
Calligraphy by Edward E. Thi

Library of Congress Cataloging-in-Publication Data

Deng, Ming-Dao.
Everyday Tao : living with balance and harmony / Deng Ming-Dao:
calligraphy by Edward E. Thi. — 1st ed.
Includes bibliographical references
ISBN 0–06–251395–8 (pbk.)
1. Taoist meditations.   2. Religious life—Taoism.   I. Title.
BL 1942. 8.D463 1996
299'.51444—dc20   96–4404

96 97 98 99 00 ❖RRDH 10 9 8 7 6 5 4 3 2 1

Contents

Introduction

Following Tao means following a living path. It is a way of life that sustains you, guides you, and leads you to innumerable rich experiences. It is a spiritual path of joy and insight, freedom and profundity.

Tao is everywhere. It is literally the movement of all life. It is endless and flows in all directions. Since Tao is the total ongoing process of the universe, it makes sense to go along with it. If we swim in a river, we should make use of its current.

The study of Tao originated in China; its history spans thousands of years. Its methods, doctrines, and practices have evolved into a sprawling and complicated system that cannot be completely grasped even with a lifetime of study. Some individuals still try. Initiates into religious Taoism, having both the calling and the opportunity, follow an arduous and devout life. But Tao flows for ordinary people and ascetics alike. After all, everyone is faced with the same struggles: the sun rises and sets on all of us, the seasons change for everyone, everyone ages. No matter who we are, the process of Tao affects us. The only question is whether we become aware of it and live in accord with it.

We all can live a life according to the principles of Tao, and we need not defer our study until some future time when we think we can enter into isolation solely for spiritual inquiry. There is nothing we do that is not part of Tao. All it takes to begin living a life in harmony with Tao is a commitment to ongoing awareness. After that, there is only the thrilling process of learning more and more about Tao.

Here are some of the special qualities of those who follow Tao:

Simplicity: Those who follow Tao keep life simple. They conserve their energies; they are content with what they have. Since they don't hanker after the dazzling goals of others who are ambitious, they are able to maintain their equilibrium.

Sensitivity: Those who follow Tao are observant of others, avoid the aggressive, and help those in need. They love nature and spend time in the wilderness learning from the seasons, studying animals, and absorbing the lessons of nature's creativity. Nature is not wholly synonymous with Tao, but it is completely a part of Tao and thus a perfect way to glimpse Tao.

Flexibility: This is the aspect of Tao people of other disciplines often have the most trouble accepting. Since Tao holds that everything in the world is relative, it does not espouse any absolutes. Followers of Tao rarely rule anything out, because they believe any choice they make is dependent upon circumstance rather than preconceived notions.

Independence: Those who follow Tao seldom care about society's dictates, fads, trends, political movements, or common morality. They find these too limited, too imperfect, and too petty. It is not that those who follow Tao are immoral. It is just that they act from a far more profound level of the spirit. For this reason, followers of Tao have often been accused of being dangerous both to religion and society. But those who follow Tao affirm wisdom and experience over government, conventional morality, and etiquette.

Focused: Those who follow Tao learn an inner direction in their lives. They accept who they are, and they first ascertain and then accept the details of their lives. They take advantage of who they are and do not try to be someone they are not. They accept that they were born, they accept that they will die, and they take the distance traveled between those two points as their personal path. They accept that each stage of their lives has certain advantages and disadvantages, and they set out to work with those advantages.

Cultivated: Since a life of Tao is one of simplicity, observation, and action, people strive to refine themselves in order to follow Tao more perfectly.

Disciplined: Those who follow Tao are disciplined. This discipline is not a harsh structure imposed upon one's personality, but the taking of orderly actions toward specific goals. That requires concentration of the highest order.

Joyous: Once one gains Tao, there is absolutely no doubt about it. It's like seeing a god, or paradise: no matter what anyone says or does, the experience cannot be erased. So too is it with those who have seen Tao and who live within its flow: They have a joyous sense of the deepest sustenance. They feel directly connected with the source of life. They do not fear tyranny, because no tyrant could ever destroy their faith in Tao. They do not fear poverty, because Tao brings them wealth overflowing. They do not fear loneliness, because Tao surrounds them constantly. They do not fear death, because they know in Tao there is no death.

Books on Tao

Those initially interested in Tao usually begin with a reading of the *Dao De Jing* (*Tao Te Ching*), by the sixth-century B.C. Taoist sage Lao Zi (Lao Tzu) in the Zhou (Chou) dynasty. From there, they may go on to the *Yi Jing* (*I Ching*), which gives insight into many of the cosmological concepts of Taoism and uses chance as a means of connecting with Tao for the purposes of divination. Those more philosophically inclined often take up *Zhuang Zi* (*Chuang Tzu*), while those interested in internal alchemy might read the works of Ge Hong (Ko Hung). Other translations commonly read are the *Art of War, The Secret of the Golden Flower,* and *The Jade Pivot*. In addition, there are numerous other volumes—academic histories, novels, and poetry—as well as works on related topics such as alchemy, herbal medicine, acupuncture, art, martial arts, longevity exercises, geomancy, ritual, and even sorcery.

But after reading all these books, then what? After reading what a sage had to say over two thousand years ago, then what? After wondering how much has been lost in the translation, then what?

Of course, we go on living our lives, confronting whatever comes our way when we go out the door. We may think of Tao while we are working. We may wonder what the sages might say while we are trying to make sense of our lives. On that there is very little written. How do we make the leap from the wisdom of ancient masters to what we must face in the here and now?

Everyday Tao has been written against the background of the books just mentioned. It has also been written from a Taoism handed down not centuries ago but in the twentieth century. It has been written with the aim of examining what is most fundamental, in the belief that the basics of Tao are also the most universal.

Indeed, in order to emphasize how much this book deals with the Tao of everyday life, the words *Taoist* and *Taoism* are generally avoided. Instead, phrases such as "the followers of Tao" are used. In place of *the* Tao, we simply say Tao. This is all by way of emphasizing that we are discussing neither the academic Tao nor the religious Tao.

Everyday Tao is not an attempt to present another interpretation of classical teachings. It is not another translation. It is a quest for Tao in contemporary times.

For this reason, *Everyday Tao* seeks to go beyond the many books already translated. It aims to penetrate classics, essays, and even sentences to the level of the very words central to Tao. It is startling to see how direct an understanding one can get from contemplating ideograms. It is amazing how abstract theory becomes superfluous when we see the origins of each idea. For example, when we truly understand what the word *Tao* shows, we can absorb its meaning without endless theorizing. Tao shows us a person on a path. That image is very simple and accessible.

If we think about it more, the idea expands. The person on the path can represent all of humanity. The person on the path can represent the universe itself. The path contains the idea of movement. We can see how everything about humanity—evolution, history, and civilization—is included in the idea of movement. We can see how the constant process of the cosmos is included in the idea of the path pictured in the word *Tao*. In short, understanding what the Chinese words picture is not only a fascinating study, but a direct and tangible way of learning. With each word, we are literally provided with a picture.

There are different styles of writing in Chinese. *Everyday Tao* goes back to the earliest, most primitive style. Many people also think it is the most beautiful. In this style, called the Small Seal Script, the pictures are simplest and most obvious. By taking a primal form of Chinese and applying it to modern life, we can span the whole history of Tao and grasp what is immediately relevant to us. Once we gain a beginning on the path, all the teachings of Tao will be that much more open to us. The ultimate goal of study is not the accumulation of book knowledge, but the immediate application of our understanding to daily life.

The Structure of *Everyday Tao*

Everyday Tao is divided into fifteen parts because these are the subjects most fundamental to any contemporary inquiry into Tao. At different points in the book, there are stories of how the earliest masters formulated their ideas about Tao. By looking at the simple situations that gave rise to their perceptions, we can see how the masters' insights were not the result of abstruse philosophical calculations, but the result of everyday life. That's what we need today: a Tao for everyday life.

The first two parts, Nature and Silence, suggest ways in which Tao is observable every day. Just as the ancients were inspired by nature to seek Tao, so too can we begin to understand Tao through the world around us. Those who follow Tao consider nature neither hostile force nor mere dumb environment to be subdued by civilization. Quite the contrary. Those who follow Tao have always considered humanity to be a part—and a subordinate part at that —of nature. Therefore, to begin on the path of Tao is to observe nature and understand that we are a part of it.

Tao would agree with other Asian spiritual systems, such as Buddhism and Hinduism, that material reality is ultimately illusory and empty. However, in contrast to these other systems, Tao holds that the realization of this emptiness—as a state of being beyond mere intellectual assertion—comes at the climax of spiritual understanding. The ancients recognized that, for the majority of our lives, we cannot function in a state of realized emptiness. Therefore, Tao may well be unique in asserting that the everyday reality we experience "on the way" to higher spiritual states is not only valid but worth working with. Everything is Tao, even what we experience before we are fully awakened in spirit. The pragmatic teachers are willing to show how everyday life can be lived to an individual's advantage and ultimately used as the basis for a spiritual life.

Thus, the next ten parts of *Everyday Tao* concentrate on what we do with this everyday life. Part Three (Books) discusses the proper role of reading and intellectual development. Part Four (Strategy) and Part Five (Movement) take as their background the profound detailing of change that has been set forth in the *Yi Jing*. They also take into account Sun Zi's (Sun Tzu's) *Art of War* (also translated as the *Art of Strategy*). Life changes and progresses in cycles long ago documented by the ancients. One of the greatest advantages of following Tao is the ability to apply these principles directly to one's own life. Along the way, of course, one is not only living a wiser life but subtly learning about Tao.

Part Six (Skill) and Part Seven (Craft) discuss the artistic aspects of Tao. The benefits of skill and craft are that one becomes self-sufficient, one becomes more sensitive, and in plumbing one's own creative depths, one gradually learns about the self.

The next four parts—Conduct, Moderation, Devotion, and Perseverance—focus on the qualities one can cultivate even if one is not yet fully cognizant of Tao. When faced with problems, we have all asked ourselves, "What is the right thing to do?" When faced with spiritual feelings, we have all asked ourselves, "How can I express myself?" And when faced with the trials of life, we have all asked ourselves, "How can we go on?" Those who follow Tao are always pragmatic. We cannot leap to heaven in a single instant, so it's good to prepare for the arduous journey.

Part Twelve looks at the all-important questions of a spiritual teacher's importance. It also discusses some of the problems of being a student.

Part Thirteen arrives at the question of the self. Although self-realization is as central to Tao as it is to many of other spiritual systems, those who follow Tao believe in *gradually* looking into the self, so that excesses and frustration are avoided. If we have become aware of our place in nature, if we have studied how the world changes and moves, if we have steadied ourselves during life's difficult times, then we can begin to consider the self.

Part Fourteen (Simplifying) speaks of one of Tao's most central concepts. After you have engaged in all the efforts of the journey, you inevitably begin to simplify. You know what you need to do to get by, and you drop what has become superfluous. You have had experiences and tested your ambitions. You have faced matters of life and death and found what worked for you and what didn't. At this stage of Tao, you begin to simplify your life. You find what is essential.

Part Fifteen (Union) finally comes to the point of direct integration with Tao. Will you emphasize union in the sense of realizing that reality is empty? Will you emphasize union in the sense that you realize you are simply a child of Tao and let Tao carry you through life? These are the questions to be resolved in the time of union.

From this brief overview, you can see that Tao is the great reality that is within nature. It urges each of us to understand our place in this world, to accept ourselves and work with who we are in relationship to each of our journeys. And most important, it always maintains this very crucial point: wherever you are on your path is always valid. All inquiry and action begin with you.

The Characters

Why is *Everyday Tao* based on the structure of Chinese characters? First of all, Tao was formulated in Chinese, and an understanding of what these characters mean helps avoid misconceptions. Second, by going back to basic words, we can try to grasp what is most fundamental about Tao.

Chinese characters can be divided into six types, a brief understanding of which will be helpful in reading this book:

Images: Simple and obvious pictures. For example, the word for "moon" is a drawing of the crescent moon.

Indicators: Characters that suggest a meaning. For example, the word for "bright" combines the symbols for the sun and the moon.

Phonetics: Symbols added to a word to indicate its sound. Sometimes the picture that forms the phonetic element has only a peripheral connection to the overall meaning of the word. For example, the word *ask* is formed by a picture of a mouth and a doorway. Although the image of someone standing in a doorway to ask a question is very strong, the main function of the door element is to give a hint as to how the word should be pronounced.

At other times, the phonetic has nothing to do with the meaning of the word. The reason for this is that oral language developed much faster than the written language. In separate localities, many words were only spoken sounds, with no written equivalents. By the time the codifiers of the language added these words to the lexicon, they had to pair a sign that represented the general meaning of the word with another that came close to the sound already in general use. Since the visual meaning and the sound were not always coincidental with the word being created, there are words in which the phonetic adds no further meaning to the character.

Combinations: Repetition of a basic image (for example, the word *many* doubles the sign for evening) or the putting together of two or more images to form a more complex picture (for example, the word for "city" shows a man holding a halberd atop the ramparts).

Derivatives: Words that allude to or are somehow reflective of other words. For example, the word for "down" is a simple transposition of the word for "up." The word for "left" shows a left hand, while the word for "right" is a mirror image, the right hand.

Borrowings: Characters that originally meant one thing but came to symbolize another concept. For example, a picture of a bird returning to its nest at sunset began to be used for "west," because the sun sets in the west.

Keeping these six structures in mind will facilitate a quick understanding of each word. You may even find yourself quite involved with the study of these characters once you know what to look for. Certainly, calligraphers, poets, artists, and scholars throughout the ages have found themselves enraptured by the beauty of these ideograms.

The Entries

Each page of this book features the following elements:

- A one-word title that corresponds to the calligraphy shown.
- The calligraphy.
- The pronunciation of the word. Except for the word *Tao,* all Chinese has been romanized using the Pinyin system.
- The definitions of the word.
- A detailed description of what is pictured in each part of the ideogram. If part of the word is a phonetic and its meaning is

not relevant to the word, the definition of that phonetic is generally omitted.

- A quick interpretation of how the word inspires some insight into Tao.
- A commentary about what we can learn about Tao in relation to the word.

The entries are purposefully short to invite you, the reader, to contemplate the ideogram directly and to consider its meaning in relation to your own personal Tao. Who you are is always right. Ultimately, your life and your relationship to Tao are solely a matter of your own spirit.

Be spiritual. Realize Tao. To do that is the most beautiful, most wonderful endeavor. We are all travelers. We are all on a journey. Some people stumble blindly along. Many follow the herd. But Tao is for those who wish to travel with awareness.

The word *Tao* shows a person on a path. That person is you. And if you learn the ways of Tao, your journey on that path will be radiant with understanding and joy.

Part One

NATURE

Tao

Dao. *Tao, way, road, path, course, head, principle, doctrine, to speak.* The character on the left means "to run." It is formed by combining the sign for "movement" (the diagonal lines) with the sign for "leg." The character on the right is a picture of a face—the vertical lines at the top represent tufts of hair, and the rectangle below represents the face.

Tao is a person running along a path.

The ancients who first taught of Tao were simple, rustic people. They formed their view by walking in granite-bladed mountains, digging in grainy soil, and sailing down wide rivers. As they worked and traveled, they slowly discerned a grand order to life. They noticed the regular phases of the sun, moon, earth, and tides. They followed the seasons. They watched the births, lives, and deaths of people, as well as the rise and fall of kingdoms.

In the nights, the ancients sat beside open fires and spoke to those who wanted to learn. As illustrations of their ideas, and to aid their students' memories, they drew pictographs in the dirt. They taught their lessons from what they had experienced: life was a movement supreme—greater than humans, greater than heaven and earth. Nothing was fixed, for everything—from the cycles of the sun and moon to the making and destroying of empires—showed endless, cyclical transformation. All this they summed up by drawing a picture of Tao: a person running along a path.

Those who want to study Tao can gain much from that simple image. It represents the organic movement of the cosmos as a great, balanced, and dynamic body in motion, just as it represents the path each of us follows through life. Sometimes intellectual definitions of Tao can be challenging. Returning to the image of Tao centers our contemplations.

Follow

Cong. *To follow, to obey.* On the left is the character for "movement." On the right are two people, one following the other.

To follow Tao is the ultimate act.

Accept Tao as the supreme description of life, the ancients urged, and life in its most spiritual form will be revealed. But even among the earliest students, doubt persisted. Should they follow Tao through flood and famine, earthquake and drought, corruption and invasion, lawlessness and banditry, fear and loneliness? Why did the path the ancients advocated still hold misfortune?

In response, the ancients stood up, walked in a circle, and then wordlessly sat back down.

This confused the students, as it may well confuse us. What the ancients were saying, in their most succinct way, was that each of us must accept and follow Tao. Good and bad are part of Tao and cannot be avoided. Rather than exhausting ourselves by striking out on our own, or worse, trying to go against the grain of life, we can come to see misfortune as part of a cycle we can both understand and utilize. But we won't learn that unless we follow Tao with complete trust.

Just as the word for "follow" shows one person following another, each of us can learn to follow Tao as if we were following a trusted friend. Then we will never be lost in the cycles of happiness and disaster.

See

Jian. *To see.* A large eye is pictured on top of a person. Without observation, learning is impossible.

When students wanted to learn of Tao, they sought out the guidance of wise elders. Learning was not formal. The ancients accepted any student they felt was sincere. Perhaps there was a simple conversation under a tree or a quiet invocation touching a rock. Then the younger one merely walked with the older one. The students wanted to see Tao. By pointing out animals and trees, leading the way through tiger-filled mountains and flower-covered valleys, fording icy rivers, and crossing sun-scorched deserts, the ancients showed the way of the world in its limitless variety.

What was so important about this method is that the ancients trusted their students to see. They trusted their students' perceptions. They didn't say, "Learn Tao from my words." They didn't say, "You are incapable of seeing Tao." They didn't say, "You can only gain Tao through elaborate rituals in temples." Instead, they simply let their students live and travel with them, and they knew that the students would see Tao in the wind and mountains, trees and rivers, animals and people. The real Tao wasn't inaccessible. The real Tao was the everyday Tao.

The idea that each of us can be directly spiritual is radical. Most religions are based not on teaching adherents to be directly spiritual, but in persuading them to trust in the intercession of ministers or priests. The problem with this approach is that we cannot gain access to spirituality except through the medium of a fallible human being. The example of the traveling students shows us otherwise: if we want to see Tao, we need only open our eyes and trust what we see.

Sky

Tian. *Sky, heaven, nature.* The topmost horizontal line represents the horizon. Below is a person with outstretched arms.

Heaven is always greater than humanity.

It was natural that the students wanted to know their place in the grand Tao. The ancients told them that this would be apparent soon enough, but the students pressed the old ones to reveal more. Then the teachers gave a lesson still given to students today.

They pointed one hand to the sky and the other to the earth.

This gesture is one of the most profound in the tradition of Tao. It places human beings between heaven and earth, but also after heaven and earth in importance (the traditional saying is "Heaven, Earth, and Humanity"). It also serves as a reminder that people are a part of all things under heaven. Even today, the world is often referred to by the phrase "below heaven."

The word *tian* means "sky," "heaven," and "nature" simultaneously. Thus, Tao was to be discerned in heaven/nature. Contemplating the sky is one way of contemplating Tao.

The sky is above us. It is endless, vast, ever present yet ever changing. It is not an abstract philosophical concept but a daily presence. The wind blows through its blue expanse. The clouds gather and disappear in its vastness. Without its air we could not breathe. Without the sun, we could not live. We can not live without the essential elements of the sky and earth.

The human spirit is great, and is not content unless it has a greatness as vast as the sky's in which to roam. We must not make our idea of Tao too small. Even though Tao shows a person along a path, it is an infinite path in an endless world.

Earth

 De. *Earth.* On the left side, the lower horizontal line represents the ground, and the cross represents a plant growing up from the ground. On the right is a phonetic.

All growth comes from the earth.

"What is bountiful?" the ancients asked. True bounty was not the treasury of the emperor, but the generosity of the earth. The golden hills provided home, country, belonging. The rich, black, fertile-smelling soil gave grain, vegetables, and fruit. The blue-shadowed mountains gave shelter from wind and storm. And the seemingly endless plains and deserts provided ample room for exploration and adventure. Why worry about the abstruse, the ancients asked, when everything we require has already been given to us?

If you want to follow Tao, the ancients said, first understand the perfection of heaven and earth. Wind, rain, and sun come to us through the sky. The earth gives us our home, our nourishment, jewels for our adornment, minerals for our use, places for travel. As the old saying goes, "Why look far away for what is close at hand?" You, like the young students of the ancients, may want to study Tao. Doing so may be as simple as bending down to pick up a clump of earth.

So many of us look and look for Tao. The masters, it seems, are still pointing one hand to the sky and the other to the earth.

Sun

 Ji. *Sun, day.* Pictured is the simple circle of what gives us light and warmth.
The sun is the power of the center.

One day, the ancients wordlessly held their hands out to the sides. The students were puzzled. When the students peered endlessly at the outstretched hands, the ancients began to laugh. It was not the hands that were important, but something the hands symbolized. The students could not guess. Finally, the teachers explained. Their left hands represented the sun, their right hands the moon.

The ancients wanted to draw attention to the sun, because it provided light and warmth. They noticed its roundness. And they said it was powerful because of the energy emanating from its center.

The ancients pointed out the farmers, who lived according to the sun. So great was the power of the sun that seeds germinated if struck by light for only a few minutes. So great was its life-giving power that entire fields ripened all over the earth. The farmers therefore followed the sun's rising and setting. They planted and harvested by the equinoxes and solstices. They knew that the sun drove the seas, made the trees live, stirred the breezes. And all because of the power of the center.

Even today we can follow the ancients' example. We know in even greater detail what the ancients could only sense: that the sun is the center of our planets, that its core is blazingly hot and bright. We can take the sun as an image to follow in our own lives. We can seek our own center, the source of our own power, and be self-sufficient. We can each strive to be as brilliant as the sun, remaining unashamed of our talents. When helping others, we can be as impartial as the sun, extending ourselves to those around us. If everyone would do that, then the light of good would truly shine upon all.

Moon

Yu. *Moon*. This is a picture of the crescent moon. The moon is constant.

It is important in life to be constant. The ancients urged their students to look at the moon. It was faithful to its course. It was the center of the night sky. For thousands of years, children, women, and men looked up to it and found inspiration and wonder.

The moon keeps to its orbit. Silently. Unwaveringly. True, it has its phases. Its course, its movement, its path in life—in short, its Tao—leads it into shadow and into brightness. Does it complain? Does it seek a different course? It does not.

Let the light that falls upon it change. Let its face sometimes be in shadow: The moon daily witnesses with its own body the play of shadow and light. It accepts that, and in so doing it uplifts all who see it.

The moon has its own primal power. It pulls on the earth; it pulls on the oceans and on the hearts and minds of human beings; it paces the seasons. The moon does not fight. It attacks no one. It does not worry. It does not try to crush others. It keeps to its course, but by its very nature, it gently influences. What other body could pull an entire ocean from shore to shore? The moon is faithful to its nature and its power is never diminished.

Look no further than tonight's sky if you would want to know how you can be both true to Tao and to yourself.

Water

 She. *Water.* The picture shows the flowing of a stream. Water is life.

When the ancients and their students stopped to rest by a pure flowing stream, the teachers compared Tao to water.

Water is flowing. Every drop is made of the same substance. Water never fears being divided, because it knows it will flow back together in time. It is eternal.

Water is powerful. Although it can be soothing, comforting, and cleansing, it can also be enormous, mighty, and overpowering. Its nature is constant. It is true to itself at any extreme.

Water is profound. In the depths of the lakes, in the darkness of the oceans, it holds all secrets. It is dangerous. It is mysterious. Yet life came from those depths.

Water is unafraid. From any height, it will plunge fearlessly down. It will fall and not be injured.

Water is balanced. No matter what the situation is, water will seek its own level as soon as it is left alone. Water will always flow downward to the most stable level. It conforms to any situation in a balanced way.

Water is nourishing. Without water, no plant and no living creature could survive.

Water is still. It can be completely still, and in its stillness, mirror heaven perfectly.

Water is pure. It is transparent, clear, needing neither adornment nor augmentation.

For all these features—to be flowing, powerful, profound, unafraid, balanced, nourishing, still, and pure—one who would follow Tao need only emulate water in every way.

Field

 Tien. *Field.* A plot of land, seen from an aerial view, is divided into different areas for plowing and planting.

   We cannot live without working the fields. We cannot know Tao without cultivating ourselves.

In the spring, the ancients went to the fields. They cleared away weeds and tilled the earth.

Everyone worked hard in the field, and the work and the sharing were good. They felt the dirt caked on their fingers and the shovel, heavy in their hands. When they scattered the seeds, they knew that some would not sprout. They understood that of those that did sprout, some would be plucked out to avoid crowding the others. Of those that remained after that, some would be destroyed by insects or animals or the weather. Only those remaining after that had any chance of ripening before being harvested

After the crops were gathered, one or two plants were allowed to continue to maturity, to grow old, to become full with seeds. When they withered and died, the future came from their dried pods.

Growing grain to eat was something that the ancients did over and over again. They did not have to teach much about the earth: they lived on it. They did not have to talk much about blessings: without the earth's bounty, they did not eat. They did not have to talk about timing: they followed the seasons in order to plant. They did not have to talk about life and death: in the mere practice of agriculture, they were immersed in that cycle. Every day, they ate grain. Every day, the lesson of Tao filled their bellies.

If we want to learn about Tao today, we need only give consideration to all that gives us the grain we eat.

Rice

Mi. *Rice, seeds.* The cross shape represents a growing plant. The four dots represent the grains of rice.

All life starts from seed. If we want to follow life, we need only follow the course of seed to seed.

The ancients held out a handful of seeds for their students to study. They said: "Without planting, there is no crop. Without cultivation, there is no harvest. Without harvest, there is no sustenance. And without humility, none of the uses of seed would be possible."

The growing of rice involves many things before we have the rice that is food. It involves the process of planting and working in concert with the elements. It involves careful tending and long patience. It involves knowing when to transplant and when to harvest. Working through all these stages requires one overriding virtue: humility. You have to bend down to till the field. You have to look down to scatter the seeds. You must stand in mud to transplant. You have to heed the seasons and weather. You need to accept accidents and storms. You must wait for ripening.

To grow rice, you cannot be proud. The ancients taught their students with just a handful of rice. They guided them through the seasons and, in so doing, taught them the way.

Each of us needs humble diligence to make our lives ripen.

Cloud

Yun. *Cloud*. The curled line represents the vapor of clouds. In later versions, the word for "rain" was added above this curled line.

Vapor, clouds high in the sky, and precious rain hidden inside, ready to fall. If we accord with the time and place, then what we need comes to us freely.

What we do in life takes labor, yes. But that labor is no good unless it happens at the right place and at the right time. If we till the soil and throw down seeds in the middle of winter, all our efforts will be for naught. Therefore, no matter how diligent we are, our efforts are wasted unless they accord with nature. This is the lesson that the ancients taught their students in the time between planting and waiting for the rain.

They watched the clouds gathering high overhead. Curling vapors filled the skies, bringing water carried up from the breathing earth. The clouds were heavy with rain, but no one knew when the liquid treasure would fall. There was only waiting.

The ancients taught that this was true for all of life: what we need will come to us as long as we work in cooperation with what is natural. That's difficult for many people to accept. They search for teachers. They wait for life to give them answers. They go forth, trying to make things happen. But that is all unnecessary. Whatever one needs for spiritual growth is always available, as the rain is a blessing for those who live natural lives.

Essence

Jing. *Essence, refinement, semen, vigor, select.* The left half of the character means "rice" or "seed." The right half of the character is a phonetic and means "pure." (This is a picture indicating the very center of a flame combined with the character for plant—purity is the very center of the flame.)

Vigor and purity are the very basis of life.

Gazing at rice, glimpsing the seeds as they sprout, lead us to contemplate our own natures: we derive our vitality from our birth.

For those who follow Tao, it is common to talk of the essence as the biochemical nature of the body. Some even say it is the body itself. The relationship between our bodies and nature, as implied by this symbol, is intimate. We eat rice to attain our essence. Our essential selves grow with vigor, as the green shoots burst from the ground. Our essence can rise pure, as the plants grow miraculously from mud and water, to feed and support us in so many ways. The mixture of these images in relation to our very physicality bears long contemplation.

Without essence, there can be no vitality or spirituality. We should acknowledge and understand how all our lofty ambitions are rooted in our physical beginnings. No matter how great the rice plants grow (some can grow ten feet, even during a flood), they remain forever rooted in the earth. No matter how great our thinking, no matter how far-ranging our spiritual power, none of our actions can be divorced from our origins, from our essence.

Hidden in the word for "essence" is a reference to purity. Hidden in the reference to purity is a reference to the power of the center. If we would attain the long life promised those who follow Tao, we would do well to understand the secrets hidden in the word for "essence."

Breath

 Qi. *Breath, vapor, energy.* Pictured is vapor rising from fermenting rice, or vapor rising from cooking rice. This character has a wide variety of meanings and applications. It can mean "breath," but its implication is not just the process of respiration. Instead, it points to the energy that breathing implies. Every human being has *qi.* The universe has *qi.* Anything with energy has *qi.*

The essence of a human being, mixed with breath, forms a vapor that is our essential energy.

To follow Tao is to follow
The breath of the world.

It is impossible to explain *qi* to those who view the world mechanically. Certainly, biologists have built an impressive body of knowledge based on dissecting organisms and finding the smallest body components. Physicists have broken matter down into particles that verge on nothingness. But where is there a way of knowing how a whole being works? Where is there a way of describing how life works? If you want Tao to be explained mechanically, it is as impossible as mechanically trying to explain the life behind breathing. But if you sense that there is a natural, breathing flow to life and you want to live in harmony with that, then Tao is for you.

The art of following Tao is all about the study of wholeness and harmony. The emphasis is on the greatness of life, not the smallness of parts. Life is viewed not as a concert of parts, but as the grand movement of the whole.

Breath is the premier indication of life. It makes sense for us to study the breath if we want to study life. Just as we breathe, all of life breathes. To follow Tao means to breathe in concert with it.

Spirit

Shen. *Spirit.* The left side of the symbol is the word "to reveal," which is used in any word dealing with the spiritual and with abstraction. It is a simplification of what was once a grouping of the words for "heaven," "sun," "moon," and "stars": ancient shamans searched the heavens for omens. Some say the right side of the character shows two hands with a rope in between (the ancients used knotted ropes before there was writing, and these became associated with divination), while others maintain that it shows two hands on either side of a sash—a reference to a standing divinity.

When the spirit is revealed, you will find out that it was always in you.

Human beings looked down at the earth when they tilled the fields. They looked up at the skies for the rain and weather that would sustain them. They also looked up for divine guidance.

Thus, considering the spirit in the midst of fields and rain is very comfortable for those who follow Tao. There is no division between the physical and the spiritual, between the natural and the divine. It is all of a whole. To embrace one is to embrace all. If the rain comes down, if the mud fills our shoes, or if we kneel down in the fields to light incense and pray—the very act of being fully *present* in our lives is spirituality enough, for being *present* is to acknowledge that everything is spiritual.

Those who follow Tao feel that our human society, and even each of us individually, is a microcosm of the universe. The same attitude that allows an acupuncturist to diagnose the entire body from taking the pulse or a diviner to see the entire universe in the cracks of a turtle shell also allows a student of Tao to search in daily life for Tao. Therefore, in these "nesting realities" the spirituality of heaven is reflected on every level.

Everything we do is Tao. Spirituality is not just "out there." It is also all around us and in us. If we understand that, no matter where we look, spiritual revelations abound.

River

Chuan. *Stream, river.* The character represents not only the simple flow of a small stream, but the greater force of several streams coming together. The shape of a flowing river as it cuts mountains and valleys is clear.

To be like water is the essential Tao.

Water is soft, yet when its force accumulates, it can level mountains. Water is clear, so when it is true to its nature, it knows the pure Tao. Water is unafraid: it will plunge thousands of feet without being destroyed. Water is accepting: it washes away filth, and yet, when it is still, it is the filth that settles, while water returns to its pure nature. Water gives life: without it, no living being could survive.

In the time of rain, the streams swell. Little rivulets become streams, small streams become rivers. Rivers flow to the oceans. The ancients taught us that we should take water as a model and allow our characters to accumulate and gather. When all the parts of our life join with each other, the force of our personality becomes great.

How is that accomplished? Through humility. The waters accumulate because they seek the lower ground. They will not hesitate to go into deep ravines or dirty places. In so doing, the waters become greater and gather together until the result is a force neither rock, nor wood, nor human being can resist. In the same way, only those who are humble can become great, because only they have accumulated the moral force it requires to be superior.

Rock

Shi. *Rock.* A stone has fallen from a cliff.

A stone can be broken, but it cannot be forced to become something it is not. Those of us who aspire to meditation need only become like a rock.

People love rocks. People worship rocks. There is something so elementally attractive about a river stone, or a rock outlined against the sky, or a stone that supports lush moss. Many of us have some rock in our homes, whether it is a rock garden, a stone wall, or pretty pebbles picked up at the beach.

Know when to be a rock. A rock is stable. It cannot be forced into being something it is not. It knows how to meditate. A rock can be a bulwark against the rain of misfortune.

Of course, those who follow Tao know how to change. Like the game of Roshando—rock, scissors, paper—you have to know when to come out with the right transformation. If you are a rock at the time when a rock is of greatest advantage, then you are superior. However, if you become a rock at a time when a rock can be crushed or wrapped, then that is a mistake. Know when to be a rock—then you might even emerge a jewel.

Tree

Mu. *Tree.* The essential parts of a tree are shown with great simplicity: below, the spreading roots; in the middle, the straight trunk; above, the branches.

Know how to use the time to grow.

A tree uses what comes its way to nurture itself.

By sinking its roots deeply into the earth, by accepting the rain that flows toward it, by reaching out to the sun, the tree perfects its character and becomes great.

Look at its leaves, which shed the water, yet divert the life-giving liquid to its roots. Look at the strength of its limbs, which can span distances far greater than any of our own limbs could. Look at its sturdy trunk—could we stand in the constantly changing seasons and be so strong? Look at its roots. How many of us are so stable?

Absorb, absorb, absorb. That is the secret of the tree. When human beings egotistically divide themselves from nature, that is a great mistake. When we divide ourselves from Tao, we are committing the greatest crime, and like all criminals, it is we who suffer the most. No, accept what life sends you. Accept how Tao flows through you, just as the tree absorbs and grows, and you will never be without Tao.

Ancient

Gu. *Ancient.* The cross shape is the word for the number ten. The bottom square represents a mouth. In the time before there was written language, wisdom was conveyed orally. What was conveyed for ten generations was therefore considered ancient.

Those who would build their character study what is ancient.

When we see old trees, it is right to think about what is ancient, for what is old has survived many seasons of both hardship and joy. To have survived signifies not simply tenacity and longevity. It also signifies being at one with Tao, for anything that grows old must be in touch with the sustaining Tao.

It is because of this that those who follow Tao study the ancient. What are the secrets of what has lasted? If we would endeavor to find wisdom beyond the mere moment, we must ask this question over and over. Whether it is an inquiry into how the shark has adapted to the changing oceans, or how the patterns of the deer's migration have changed with the climate, or how a redwood has adapted to fires and winds, or how a craftsperson has learned to use traditional motifs in new ways, we can learn how to make our own actions lasting and meaningful.

To study the reverse is also valuable. We can easily see how ancient things that lost their touch with Tao were destroyed. Why did the dinosaurs disappear from this planet? Where are the invading hordes of Mongols now? How did our language leave behind outmoded expressions? Studying how ancient things crumbled is also important.

Not to ape the ancient, and yet to revere the ancient—that is the secret to the superior person's learning.

Mountain

Shan. *Mountain*. Pictured are peaks outlined against the sky.

To go up the mountains, away from people and closer to heaven, is the path to Tao.

The ancient teachers took their students to the mountains, so that they could find inspiration in the high, sweeping vistas. Each of them could take pleasure in the fresh air scented with pine and herbs. None of them could fail to clear the mind of the toil and considerations of daily life. From ancient times to the present, the mountains have been the best places to learn about Tao.

The ancients believed that there was something called the mountain spirit. They took pains to emphasize to their students that they should not confuse this spirit with the demons and hobgoblins of childhood stories. The mountain spirit was one of purity and isolation. Even though Tao was everywhere, spiritual wisdom was too easily lost in the cares and considerations of the plains. In the isolation of the mountains, with the voices of the throng stilled, the whispers of Tao could finally be heard. This was what the ancients called the mountain spirit.

Sometimes certain students wanted to study Tao longer. They became so enthralled with the whispers of the mountain spirit that they stayed there and learned of Tao without any of the distractions of society. These were the great people of Tao, for they became imbued with the mountain spirit.

Tiger

Hu. *Tiger.* Here the essential elements of the tiger are quite apparent: the rearing, sinewy body ending in a curling tail, the pouncing paws, open jaws, and pointed ears.

Once we awaken to Tao, the force of our own spirit will be as strong as a tiger's.

When we learn to tap into the power of Tao inside ourselves, we will feel a vitality as strong as a tiger's. That is pure energy. It is very important to direct that power positively.

There were plenty of evil Taoists in history. Even in ancient times, there were men and women who grasped the essential principles of life, mastered psychology and politics, and learned how to safeguard their health. They used these skills not for spiritual purposes, but to enslave others, topple kingdoms, and seek immortality. They were like killing tigers.

There were, of course, many good people among the ancients as well. These people also understood the way of heaven, understood how to preserve life, and looked deeply into the soul. They used their skills to teach others, spread contentment, and cultivate enlightenment. Their spirits were even more indomitable than those of the evil Taoists. They were like noble tigers.

In the legends of Tao are tales of tigresses who rescued children, giving them their own milk and raising them in the wild. We who follow Tao and gain access to its power must be like the tigresses— combining ferocity with nurturing.

Crane

Guan. *Crane.* The two eyes of the crane and its feathers are well shown. The crane is so strongly identified with the idea of stillness that the modern form of the word also means "contemplation."

Everything we need to know about vigilance can be learned from the crane.

Sometimes, on a high cliff, the ancients pointed out the proud profile of the crane.

When the crane made a certain call, the ancients knew that rain was approaching—how wise the bird was, though it never read the classics.

The crane could stand for hours on one leg—how strong it was, even though its legs were thin.

The crane flew to mountain lakes, waded in the waters, and waited patiently until it caught a fish—how observant it was.

The crane masterfully combines vigilance and movement. Those are exactly the qualities we need to go through life and to follow Tao. Vigilance is hard to get right. All too often we confuse vigilance with passivity—we are willing to wait and look, but we forget to act. Vigilance is not a matter of mere waiting. It is a matter of the correct timing. It takes an exquisite sense of proportion to know that we are not just standing still—we are moving no faster and no slower than required by the situation.

Carp

Li. *Carp*. The left side of the word is the symbol for "fish" (the head is pointing up, the crossed lines are the fins and scales, the bottom is the tail). The right side is a phonetic and means "village."

Those who couple wisdom and valor are inevitably successful.

The carp is a symbol of valor and strength. It will jump up rapids, swimming strongly. Carp live for a very long time, and it is not unusual for villages to have some "grandfather" fish—large, strong, mysterious, and at home in the waters since the oldest human can remember. It is no wonder that, when people saw carp jumping up cataracts, the fish came to represent success.

It's important for us to have goals and to strive toward them with the valor and the determination of the carp. Those of us who have goals have meaning and direction in our lives. Notice that the direction need not be with everyone else. Just as the carp will swim against the current to reach its goal, so too must we know when we must stand up to fate in order to be successful. Just as the carp strives by its own strength, not depending on others, so too must we be capable of marshaling our deepest reserves when the time comes. It is too facile to say that the way to follow Tao is to simply go along with the flow of life. Sometimes, like the carp, we must know when to go it alone.

Needless to say, it is critical for us to have good judgment and inner reserves. Blind courage is useless. Throwing ourselves bodily at a problem is to mistake brute force for valor. Such actions inevitably exhaust us rather than produce the triumph that the carp teaches. The carp shows us how: a carp never closes its eyes and so is ever wakeful. It never stops swimming, and so is always acting.

Turtle

Guei. *Turtle, tortoise.* This is one of the easiest pictures to see. The shell is in the center, feet on the left and right, and head above. Since ancient script was written on narrow strips of bamboo and other materials, there wasn't enough room to portray animals horizontally. That is why the word for "turtle" appears to be standing on end.

In ancient times, the turtle shell was a tool for divination. That is why Zhuang Zi's question to the two officials regarding the sacred tortoise is all the more poignant.

One of the ancients of Tao, Zhuang Zi, was fishing when two imperial courtiers came to him. The emperor wanted Zhuang Zi to become a high official. Zhuang Zi said to the courtiers, "There is an ancient turtle shell in the imperial temple used by the national priests for divination. Do you think the turtle would rather be highly venerated or dragging its tail in the mud?" The officials replied, "We suppose that he would rather be dragging his tail in the mud." At that, Zhuang Zi burst out, "Go away then, and let me drag my tail in the mud!"

We all know the fable of the tortoise and the hare and the obvious lesson we're supposed to draw from it. Sadly, the world has changed. The fable assumed a finish line that didn't move. Lately, it seems that we're always chasing a moving target in life. All things are in flux, and life doesn't give us the luxury of a finish line that will wait. If we are to learn the lesson of the tortoise, it would be that we must have self-sufficiency, endurance, protection, and perseverance. But if we don't combine those with other qualities, we can never move fast enough in this shifting world.

Unless we're like Zhuang Zi's turtle in the mud.

Part Two

SILENCE

Immediate

 Cai. *To present, now.* The character on the left represents "silk" and shows two cocoons with silk thread. The word on the right means "the deep color of the head of a bird." This word is a reference to a piece of silk that had been dyed to its deepest color. Once a piece of silk had reached this color, it was quickly presented for inspection, and so the later meanings of "immediate" and "presenting" were attached to the word.

To simply be ourselves is the greatest challenge but the simplest spiritual technique.

A piece of silk, while it is in the dyeing vat, does not think of being anything other than a piece of silk. It absorbs the dye, and nothing can hasten the process. To deepen the color, the silk must again be immersed in the vats. We who seek Tao are like silk being dyed. We immerse ourselves in Tao, and we absorb Tao. But our essential nature will not change, just as the substance of the silk is not changed by dyeing. Nor is our essential nature in need of any change. Like the silk that is brought out and presented, we are who we are, and there is no reason to be ashamed of that. That is why we can be immediate in everyday life: we know who we are, and we trust in the process of Tao.

Thus, the ancients taught their students to always accept themselves as they were. This is not only eminently practical—to do otherwise is ultimately impossible—but it is the beginning of the attitude of acceptance that we need to follow Tao. If we cannot accept ourselves, it is unlikely that we will be able to accept anything that Tao sends our way.

By accepting ourselves, we can then bring great immediacy to our lives.

Open

 Kai. *Open.* The word depicts the two leaves of a door, with two hands taking away the bar.

In learning, we should remove whatever bars our way.

There is no curse on humanity. There is no original sin. There is no bad karma from previous transgressions. There is no spiritual wisdom forbidden to people. The true spiritual downfall of humanity occurs only when people ignorantly and willfully close themselves to spiritual wisdom.

Those who put up walls and a gate and shut themselves away soon find that they have become ingrown and fearful of the world. Disease and stagnation heap up, and no good fortune comes their way. It is only when the doors of a home are open that clean air flows in, guests come to visit, and the melodious sounds of birdsong float in.

A person's mind is like a great house. Those who keep their minds closed cut themselves off from the live-giving vitality of Tao. Conversely, those who want Tao open themselves to it and so find an influx of great energy.

The two leaves of each person's door are ignorance and selfishness. The ignorant think they know everything, and so they are not open to anything new. The selfish cannot think beyond themselves, and so they do not have the farsighted qualities needed to understand Tao. The wise open their doors wide and let the vitality of Tao flow freely.

Constancy

Chang. *Constancy, rule, principle, usual, general, ordinary.* The upper part of the word is a phonetic and is a picture of a house. The bottom part is a banner. The banner is constantly floating in front of a general's headquarters.

Great constancy is the best way to follow Tao.

Make no mistake: Tao is always here.

Tao is like the banner in the word *chang.* The general may not notice the flag, but the wind that stirs it is still there. In the same way, we may not always be aware of Tao, but we can sense its effects on every part of our lives. That is why Tao is called constant.

The ancients urged us to open ourselves and be aware of Tao at all times. They did not want us to think of it only when we were in a temple. They did not want us to read the classics and ignore them in our daily lives. They wanted us to open the doors of our house and never close them to the fresh breeze of Tao.

If we are like the general who comes to his door, throws it open, sees the banner that shows the constant Tao, and breathes in the clean wind that comes his way, then the rest of Tao is not far behind.

Window

Chuang. *Window.* Above is the symbol for "cave." Below is a picture of a latticework window. (Many ancient settlements were in caves; the inclusion of the cave symbol indicates how old this character is. Caves are still common and favorite meditation places.)

Without looking out of the window, I can know the way of heaven.

Without going out of the door, I can know all things on earth.
Without looking out of the window, I can know the way of heaven.
The wise person knows others by observing himself.

Without going out of the door, I can know all things on earth.
Without looking out of the window, I can know the way of heaven.
The wise person will not go out when fate is in opposition.

Without going out of the door, I can know all things on earth.
Without looking out of the window, I can know the way of heaven.
The wise person knows when to withdraw into contemplation.

Without going out of the door, I can know all things on earth.
Without looking out of the window, I can know the way of heaven.
The wise person uses experience as a guide.

Without going out of the door, I can know all things on earth.
Without looking out of the window, I can know the way of heaven.
The wise person knows that what must truly be open is the mind.

Above

 Shang. *Above, upper, superior, to mount, upon.* The horizontal line represents the earth, and the line above logically points upward.

We must be receptive to what is above—Tao—not the social world.

Rain pours from above. Snow falls from above. The winds blows from above. The sunlight shines from above. The stars sparkle above. The moon glows above. We who must be open to Tao must also be receptive to what is above.

It is to the Tao of heaven that we must remain constantly open. We cannot similarly put our trust in society. Since ancient times, dynasties have risen and fallen. Tyrants have oppressed millions. Despots have ruined their countries with taxes and conscription. Petty philosophers have confused people with their sophistry. Temples have become centers of corruption. Life in this world is all too easily won or lost. Therefore, we should not open ourselves to the vagaries of humanity, but rather to the impartial power of Tao.

Heaven, it is said, preaches not of benevolence. In fact, heaven does not speak at all. Heaven is not a place of gods. Heaven is impartial. It takes no sides. It neither helps nor hinders human endeavors. It is consciousness without partiality. And therefore, it is supremely spontaneous, supremely powerful, and supremely creative. That is the Tao that the ancients would have us open ourselves to: not a world of human scheming, but a world of heavenly purity.

Purity

Qing. *Pure, clear, clean.* The sign for "water," on the left, alludes to its transparency. The rest of the word is a phonetic; from the idea of the color at the base of a flame, it extrapolates the meaning of "purity."

To be with Tao, we need only innocence.

Purity is the ultimate Tao. It is like clear running water. Or newly fallen snow. Or a freshly sprouting plant in early spring. Or a newborn child. Purity is real, and it is the state of Tao.

Innocence is to be absolutely clear, without the taint of selfishness. Innocence knows no ulterior motives, no lust for immortality, no drive to be extraordinary. Innocence is simplicity.

The ancients taught that you are already innocent. No matter who you are, you have an inviolable core. No matter how many sins you have committed, there is a part of you that is pure. The ancients deeply believed this of all human beings.

It is from this core that you should seek Tao. It is not necessary to seek Tao in an intellectual way, or in an ambitious way, or in a selfish way. It is unnecessary to seek Tao for the sake of some supposed salvation. If you understand your own absolute purity, then you can see how unnecessary such methods are. You are already pure.

Innocence does not need to make efforts. Innocence does not need to belong to groups. Innocence does not need to be anything. Innocence is inherently pure, and that inherent purity is Tao.

White

 Bai. *White*. The outside circle is an indication of a cavity; the line within indicates that there is nothing there. By extension, this means "white," the absence of anything inside. Another interpretation is that this is a picture of a white silkworm cocoon.

It is white inside each of us.

White is the symbol for purity. In ceremonies, it is given as the color of spirituality.

Since the ancients taught that we are already pure, they laughed at the teachers who advocated penitence and self-mortification as spiritual methods. They said: "We are already holy. Why struggle to become something we already are?"

The masters of penitence argued that we need to refine ourselves, to cleanse away disgusting desires to arrive at the pure soul inside.

The ancients replied: "If a prince dresses in different clothes, does that change the fact that he is a prince? You are already Tao. Why be so stupid as to obscure yourself when you were born complete?"

The masters of penitence declared: "Humans are evil. Humans are filled with greed. Even the innocent child is corrupted in this ocean of suffering. Let us practice holiness, so that we can return to the pure state."

The ancients only smiled and said: "If we take up a stone and rub and rub, can we make it into a diamond?"

"Not if it wasn't a diamond to begin with," the masters of penitence admitted.

With that, the ancients walked away.

Matter

Shi. *Matter, affair, to serve, office, work, duty.* On the top is a hand holding something. There is another hand below trying to get what the top hand is holding. By extension, when more than one person wants something, it becomes an important matter.

The most important matter is that of following Tao.

Our first duty is to follow Tao.
Everything else is diversion and triviality.
What matters most is to ascertain the basic:
Life, death,
And the line that connects them: Tao.

A seed contains the entire plant.
At birth, no part of you was missing.
Sun, rain, earth, and wind affect the seedling,
Just as fate affects each of us,
But in neither case is true nature altered.

We forget we were once seeds,
And we confuse the path from birth to death.
To become aware is the greatest duty,
To understand is what matters.
True wisdom goes beyond the limits.

Silence

Jing. *Stillness, silence.* On the left is the word for "purity" (see p. 31). On the left is the phonetic meaning "competition" through the depiction of two wrangling hands. The word for "purity" also implies clarity and transparency and, by extension, here means that the competition on the right is diminished to nearly nothing.

Stillness comes when there is a cessation of competition.

From ancient times to the present, people have worshiped gods. But from ancient times to the present, the tradition of Tao has taught us to look beyond the gods. What is beyond the gods? A wise person once said: "Beyond the gods is silence."

But to say we must first seek the gods and then go beyond the gods to silence can be quite discouraging. How will we, with our faults and problems, ever get to the level of gods, let alone what is beyond the gods?

Fortunately, the remark itself shows us the way. The state beyond the gods may well be silence, but can't we have silence right now? No, let's not worry about spirituality and the classics and all the rituals and great methods. Let's put all that aside. Let's stop talking—oh, that is already a big accomplishment!—and let's stop thinking—tough, but a good challenge—and let's just try to be very quiet. Let's try to be quiet for just a second. Really and totally quiet. Try to extend that to two seconds. Then a minute, and then longer and longer.

Let's not worry right now about how long that quiet is. We should not be competitive here. Let's just focus on that quiet. If "beyond the gods is silence," then in one moment of quiet, you have experienced Tao firsthand. Without a priest. Without a master. Without years of study. You have experienced for yourself the silence that is Tao.

Sit

Tso. *To sit, to meditate.* The image shows two people sitting face to face on the ground. When one first learns to meditate, one sits facing one's master, just as the two people are doing here.

Meditation is simply to sit on the ground.

There is no fancy word for "meditation." Although the ancients taught that meditation was essential, they simply called it "sitting." And they simply sat on the ground—not on the exalted furniture of civilization—but on the plain earth, which gives to us unreservedly.

At the end of long days laboring in the fields or after a long day of walking in the mountains, the ancients sat alone and in the quiet. They had endured the harshness of nature and also benefited from the abundance of nature. Rest was needed, but contemplation was also needed. It helped to absorb the passage of time. It helped to settle the turmoil of working. It helped to return to the silent purity that was Tao.

Even today, to sit and to be still is all we need for meditation. Elaborate means have been developed, but that is because the psychology of "civilized" people has become complex. The ancients knew that meditation did not need to be complicated. That is why they didn't even bother to give it a special name. It was only sitting, as anyone does after a long day. In the end, we don't need anything more than that to engage in the profundity of meditation.

Tao is always here for us. It was never any different. We only need to take the time to be silent to realize it once again.

Part Three

BOOKS

Book

Zhai. *Book*. This is a picture of strips of bamboo bound together with threads—a type of book that predated bound paper books by a great many years. Mastering books is part of mastery of Tao.

There once was a cave reopened by an earthquake. It had been hidden for centuries under vines and rocks. When the ancients explored the cave, they found a skeleton clothed in robes no longer in style. On the walls were words and diagrams. Clutched in the hand of the late master was a book. When the ancients opened the fragile leaves, they saw that all the words had been written by hand. The calligraphy was forceful and clear, so powerful that they could still see the vitality of the author in the thick flow of ink. They reverently read the book—the summation of an entire lifetime devoted to Tao—and they wept over the profundity of the words.

The knowledge derived from this sacred book allowed the ancients to gain new insight into Tao. After all, there was a special value to be gained from a person's looking back upon the whole of his life. What the ancients learned from that book was a new way of looking at things, different from the prevailing thought of that time.

The First Emperor understood how important books were. He burned books and buried scholars in order to dominate the country. Every despot since then has known that control of knowledge is control of a nation. But it didn't work for the First Emperor, and it will never work for any despot. There will always be books—which can be hidden, which need no technology to open, which are not virtual but real objects. Those who use them will not give them up easily.

That is why, even today, books are so revered. Books allow people to think for themselves, allow access to knowledge forgotten or even out of favor with the times. Books allow knowledge to travel over time and distances greater than the author could ever accomplish in person. Most important, books encourage allegiance not to kings, but to the learning of the individual. And that is crucial to Tao.

Literature

Wen. *Writing, script, literature, civil* (as opposed to military), *cultured, cultivated.* This is a picture of a person standing very solemnly—originally this word meant a dignified and serious person. It was gradually borrowed to mean all things cultural.

Those who can read the patterns of life are the truly cultured.

Every person who has followed Tao has been a person of culture and refinement. Not only does Tao require study and intelligence, but it also demands the subtle mind of a sensitive person. You will not find that type of mind in the unthinking brute or the insensitive lout.

The *wen* person is someone who can read not just human language, but the languages of nature as well. There are patterns and secrets throughout the world—the rings of trees, and tracks of animals, and the traces of water down the sides of a valley are as clear as any scripture. The person who follows Tao does not blindly go through life, but is able to read it on every level. Those who follow Tao are those who know the many languages of life.

A person who can read literature in this extended sense cannot help but develop great character. After all, to follow Tao requires patience in adversity, great compassion, and understanding of the balance between action and stillness. We all need to experience more and more, strive to know life on deeper and deeper levels, and give consideration to all that happens to us. Such understanding must be ongoing, and those who revel in *wen* never tire of exploring what is around them. They always read the patterns of life.

Classic

Jing. *Classic, scripture, to pass through.* The left half of the word represents "silk." The right half is a phonetic meaning the warp of a piece of cloth. Originally, this word may have meant something growing from the earth, or it may have represented the watercourses of the earth. It was eventually borrowed to mean the warp of cloth and then, by extrapolation, "structure" and "substance." Some people therefore interpret the word *jing* by saying the classics show us how to study and cultivate our inner substance.

To study the classics is to study the threads that bind all knowledge.

The classics are of great value. No matter how much you studied in school, the body of classics in any one culture is already greater than what one person can absorb. We should avail ourselves of that very powerful body of knowledge. Certainly, we will have more time to be creative and to explore the spontaneous wonder of Tao if we are not unknowingly moving in ruts well worn by previous generations. How can we truly be individual and original if we haven't looked to see what others have done before us?

Isn't it better to stand on the shoulders of the previous generations? That takes learning. Rather than reinvent everything, it might be better if we first learned to do things the classic way. That would be like someone who wanted to start a farm going to study the watercourses: what they found could literally determine the success of their venture. Or it would be like someone who wanted to make a tapestry: not only would he have to know weaving, but he would have to analyze the pattern to be woven right down to the threads that composed it.

That's the type of thoroughness we need when studying the classics. But we mustn't make the opposite mistake and never do anything with our knowledge. A person can wait for years next to a watercourse, but if she never drinks, she never benefits. Another person can sit with spools of thread, but if he never weaves, he will never be warm. Learn, yes. But utilize the classics as a part of your life.

Speech

 Yen. *Speech, words.* The square at the base of the character represents a mouth. The top is an expression of the remainder of the face.

Without sound, speech, and words, there would be little communication and no learning.

In ancient times, people so revered words and paper that they tried never to throw them away. When they could no longer write on a piece of paper, they carefully gathered it up and burned it reverently, so that the words and the paper could be recycled into the great process of life. There were even people who patrolled the streets to pick up paper and take it to be recycled or burned in honored places. Such was the respect people had for words.

Before the ancients spoke, they stopped to consider what they were about to say. They washed their mouths with clean water, they inhaled the air of Tao, they paused once more for contemplation. For them, words were sacred, the hard-won repositories of knowledge. They were not to be devalued by gossip or thoughtlessness.

It is natural, then, that we learn neither to waste words, nor to use them with malicious intent. If we want to be pure of spirit, we must be pure of speech. If we acquire the habit of always meaning what we say, then we have the possibility of being pure not just in speech but in character as well.

Listen

Ting. *To listen, to hear, to understand.* The upper left quadrant shows the character for "ear." The lower left quadrant shows a man standing still to listen carefully. On the right is a phonetic, the character for "virtue."

To truly listen is to perfect one's own virtue.

Just as we should be sparing and careful in speech, so too should we be careful in listening. The range of what life has to offer in listening is wide. For example, we can listen to gossip, trivialities, or obscenities. These are all words created to entertain and stimulate base sensibilities. By contrast, words of wisdom also exist, but these are too often overlooked.

The words of the wise are not all written with invisible ink on sacred books hidden in impenetrable Himalayan caves. They are widely available all over the world, even on newsstands. The secrets of life are not obscured. The sacred words are very close. But do you hear them? Do you seek them out? Do you respect them?

Listening takes time. You have to take the time to hear, but it also takes time for the words to penetrate into your heart. Just because you hear words of wisdom doesn't mean that you are instantly transformed. Therefore, those who seek Tao constantly seek words of wisdom and allow them to accumulate deep in themselves. That is why the ancients always said it takes a person of virtue to hear words of virtue. It takes a person of strength to want words of strength. It takes a person of learning to discern words of learning.

Learn

Xue. *To learn.* The upper portion represents "teacher" by two hands holding a stick. The character below is the word for "child."

Learning represents shaping and exchange.

Describe something, and one quarter of the people will understand.

Show something, and half the people will understand.

Describe something while showing it, and three-quarters of the people will understand.

Describe something, show it, and then encourage people to put their knowledge to immediate use, and nine people out of ten will understand.

If our learning about Tao is this thorough, then we will advance rapidly in our knowledge. When we read the classics, we shouldn't regard them as mere theory. The classics of Tao were written to convey information, not obscure it. Therefore, we should indeed study long and hard, with the full intention of putting any understanding of Tao to immediate use and avail ourselves of all that learning has to offer.

It is a great pity that so much false knowledge is taught to each generation. When this happens, people must spend a great deal of time undoing misconceptions and emotional conflicts inflicted by small-minded and ill-qualified teachers. That is why, from ancient times to the present, those who follow Tao take care to seek out the best teachers: by learning from the best, they enhance their chances of becoming the best.

Knowing

 Shi. *To know, to recognize, to keep in mind.* On the left is the sign for "word." In the middle is the sign for "sound." On the right is the sign for "sword." Orders are given to go to war, and the people therefore *know* their duties.

Knowledge is not just intake, but the integration of information into one's very being.

From any remote spot, one can access *information* electronically: the library at Oxford, interactive exchanges about mathematics, the latest news from anywhere in the world is immediately at hand. But this is not the same as *knowledge.*

We have answering machines, fax machines, and e-mail. But people seem to be not so much communicating as dumping. As long as they have sent a message, they feel absolved of all responsibilities with a minimum of inconvenience, social contact, or feedback.

The ancients had a very different attitude toward knowledge. Many of them were swordsmen and, as the word *shi* implies, they had to truly know the sword before they were ready to stake life and death on it. The ancients taught that one did not truly know something until that knowledge was part of one's very own soul. So before they ever ventured out with a sword, the swordsmen trained to put skill into the fiber of their muscles. Then they trained further, until their skill became part of their reflexes. Then they trained even more, until their skill became intrinsic to their minds. Then they emptied their minds, so that their skill was part of their spirit. Only then would they say that they knew enough to go to battle.

What is knowing today? True, we have an unprecedented amount of information available on an unprecedented scale. But the resolutions to the true questions of life come not through mere communications, no matter how quick or how vast. They come from knowing itself. And knowing comes only when we have made the answers part of ourselves.

Write

Shu. *To write, book.* The upper part of the word shows a hand holding a stylus. The bottom part of the word is a phonetic.

We cannot underestimate the power of the word.

Is there any spiritual system without the word? In any number of spiritual practices—from the sacred syllables of tantric yoga to the mysticism of the Kabbalah, from the Word of the Christian God to the talismanic writings of Taoist magicians—the word is central. To write is a sacred act.

All sacred calligraphers try with greater and greater effort to release the writing that is within them. This takes years of spiritual practice, like waiting for the perfect confluence of heavenly bodies. Only here the calligraphers are waiting for the confluence of skill, technique, and spontaneity to express their devotion. When they succeed, there is a state of euphoria that manifests itself in ink. This type of writing cannot be achieved by the mere normal, rational ways of a scribe. It must be inspired: one must give oneself over to a sacred feeling welling from deep within.

It takes a strong person—perhaps even an extraordinary person—to stand by what he or she has written without doubt or eagerness for recognition. If you breach the spiritual in writing, it will transform you, not in a way that will bring you profit, but in a way that will instill a great and private faith. To feel that is to feel Tao. To feel that is worth all the words in the world.

Stylus

Yu. *Stylus.* This is a picture of a hand (the top part of the word) holding a writing instrument (the vertical line) as it writes a line (the lower horizontal line) on a tablet (the upside down U shape).

If you have any doubt that you change and evolve, look at your handwriting.

The writing of adults looks nothing like the perfect examples given to schoolchildren to copy. In fact, children often need letters from adults read to them, so different are the cursive forms.

When children learn to write, their handwriting is very similar to the models. By the time they reach middle age, their handwriting has changed drastically. Perhaps time grows shorter, pressures become greater, and soon our writing becomes twisted into a nearly illegible scrawl, devoid of regularity, inconsistent in angle, rushed in its strokes. If you ask someone to write the way they did twenty years ago, they will not be able to move their hand in the same way.

We all change. To the degree that our handwriting changes, so too do our personalities change. We can look at our signature from a decade ago and wonder over the person who wrote it. But we cannot go back. Best to accept it as it is, even as it is best to accept who we have become in life.

Drum

Gu. *Drum.* In the lower left quadrant is the drum on its stand. The horizontal line above it represents the head, and the three lines at the top represent ornaments. On the right is the symbol for a hand holding a stick.

When one beats a drum, the sound is instantaneous. When one makes an inquiry, the answer should be just as quick.

For some centuries, the practice of calligraphy had become over-burdened by tradition and academic standards. Then, toward the end of the last century, ten stone drums dating from 770 B.C. were discovered in a remote area. These ten stone drums were carved with an ancient form of calligraphy (similar to the style of calligraphy used in this book). The writing had a sense of proportion and stroke that was unknown at the time they were discovered. When calligraphy needed revitalization, these words from the past, done in a style so primitive as to be fundamental, opened the way to fresh and powerful insights.

When one needs guidance, one should similarly search for the responses that will herald new understanding. Just as these stone drums woke up the world of calligraphy, so too can consulting the right person sound the exact notes you need.

Ten stone drums: they make the soundless sound. They contain hundreds of words. They lasted throughout centuries, obscure, until the moment their knowledge was needed. They have guided generations. Truly, what faith and foresight the ancient makers of these ten drums must have had!

Dictionary

Dian. *Dictionary, records, laws.* This is a picture of bamboo books placed on a high table altar.

To have the words to describe something is part of the way in which we learn.

A writing teacher once insisted: "If you can name it, you can know it." That may be true, but we must also know how to name that which cannot be named. To know the named and to know the unnamable—that is the crux of following Tao.

If you think back over your youth, you can probably remember times when something was not understandable until you found a name for it. "What is this called?" you probably asked. Or, when you asked if such-and-such a thing existed, someone probably replied, "Of course it does. It's called . . ."

The same is true of the study of Tao. We need to know the names for certain ideas and observations. By putting a name on what we sense to be right, we can then go on to define and explore it further. The exciting discovery of Tao proceeds from first hearing its name and continues through the litany of its cogent ideas.

But Tao also observes that parts of life have no names. The most profound levels of life are so enormous, so deep, and so mystical that they are unnamable. When we are dealing with this most difficult and yet most meaningful part of Tao, we have to accept that there are no words in our dictionary to define our experiences. That is why there is the phrase "Those who know do not speak." The absolute deepest part of Tao can be known, but it cannot be described.

So we must be thorough in our studies. The part of life that is named and in dictionaries must be intensely explored. But that is only half the study of Tao. We must go further, and understand what will never be listed in a dictionary. That is the unnamable, and the ultimate, Tao.

Image

Xiang. *Like, image, to resemble, elephant.* On the left is the character for "person." The right half is actually a picture of an elephant; the trunk is the hook on the top, the boxy shape is the large skull, and the remaining lines represent body and legs. It was borrowed to mean "image," possibly due largely to a phonetic coincidence.

Like the parable of the blind men trying to describe the elephant, each time we try to learn by image, we are confronting an approximate truth.

It's hard not to use metaphors. As we try to negotiate more and more complicated subjects, we resort to metaphors to aid understanding. Study of Tao is no different. We say Tao is *like* a river or *like* the flow of heaven. But, of course, those are descriptions and not Tao itself. The only intellectual way we have to describe the infinite is through the imperfect vehicle of the metaphor.

Could anyone ever believe in an elephant through mere words? The descriptions would sound wildly improbable. How could a nose also be like a snake and also like a hand? And those ears as large as big tent flaps? And its size bigger than a house? And its strength greater than ten horses? And a gray hide thicker than the heaviest leather? So unbelievable! Yet we all know elephants exist. Before we went to see our first one, those accompanying us probably used many persuasive phrases and unusual descriptions. But once we saw one, we were free to make up our minds ourselves.

That is the same way that we should use the metaphor. It's good enough to lead us to see the elephant. But once we are face-to-face with the real thing, it's up to us to grasp the truth directly.

Scholar

Shi. *Scholar, gentleman, sage, officer, soldier.* This word is a combination of the number ten above (the cross shape) and the number one (the single base line). Originally this word meant "important matters," because in court the important matters were numbered one to ten. Confucius said that great scholars were the "ones who took care of" the "ten" important matters—and therefore Confucius borrowed this word as their designation.

One who follows Tao loves scholarship.

There is something wonderful about being a lover of books. Those who follow Tao have always taken great delight in learning. They worked in the libraries, they were wandering poets, they kept official histories, and they searched the frontiers for more knowledge. The masters spent their entire lives gathering, preserving, and studying the ancient classics. Amid the constant warring and dynastic clashes it was their devotion that makes our learning possible today.

Those who follow Tao are constantly interested in new knowledge. Obscurity is not a deterrent. Detail is thrilling. Pursuit of the esoteric is an excitement. And long investigation is a pleasure. There is a saying: "Sailing on the ocean of knowledge, you can never reach the shore." The followers of Tao are happy to be sailing that way, and they probably aren't even looking for shore.

In public, perhaps at lectures, true scholars of Tao make no show of themselves. They do not parade their considerable knowledge. They sit and listen, delighted to appreciate someone else's scholarship, always respectful of the deep thoughts of others, and always willing to indulge in the pleasure of learning. When they teach, they truly share—and sometimes they forget themselves in their enthusiasm. That is all right, for scholarship is the most honorable of passions.

Poetry

Shi. *Poem, song, hymn.* On the left is the symbol for "words." On the right is a phonetic, the symbol for "temple."

Poetry is worship with words.

Even in temples
Where residents vow never to talk,
And silence is worshiped,
There is sound.
There are songs.
There is poetry.

Memories incarnated,
Lifetimes pulled through a thousand minds,
Cadences beating time,
Rhymes connecting life,
Stanzas stacked like the generations.

Those who follow Tao write poetry.
Read poetry.
Live poetry.
And enter Tao through its lines.

Sing

 Chang. *To sing.* These are three different signs for the mouth and therefore imply a group of people singing. A singer of the highest level transcends the self.

You sing.
But did that song come from you?
You have a voice, but is that your voice?

Does the painter's brush move because of the painter?
Does the writer create the text?
Is the dancer dancing?
Or the boxer fighting?

You sing, and there is a song crafted out of all you have learned from your teachers. But through all singers, once in a while, comes a song that is not the song written on the score, that has nothing to do with technique, breathing, or voice projection. It has nothing to do with being a famous singer, or standing in front of an orchestra, or performing for an audience. Sometimes a pure and divine song will come, and the singers know that this song did not come from them, but from some great and mystical source. Every singer who has felt this knows what Tao is like.

You meditate.
But is it really you meditating?

Part Four

STRATEGY

Martial

Wu. *Martial, military, warlike.* The left side is the sign for "leg" and also means "to stop." The rest of the character is a representation of a halberd. A man is standing in a firm stance and brandishing his weapon.

The greatest taming of the martial is to tame one's character.

There was once a good king of an ancient country suddenly attacked by another state. The king found his armies weak. Desperate, he called his most trusted general out of retirement. In spite of his age, the loyal General Yang rode forth with his six sons.

In those days, generals fought personally. They believed that it was their skill, coupled with the righteousness of their cause, that determined the outcome. General Yang and his sons challenged the enemy, believing that they exceeded their foe both in skill and virtue.

Tragically, the brave general was trapped in an ambush. Not wanting to disgrace his liege, he committed suicide by dashing his head against a stone. When he died, he did not know that his own prime minister—bribed by the enemy—had betrayed him. In later battles, all the sons but one were killed because of betrayal.

With all the men gone, the old general's wife led the women of the family out to fight. They were trained in martial ways too, and there were no gender distinctions in righteousness. So great was the commitment of the family to their king and so skilled were the women generals, that they finally prevailed over both the traitor and the enemy.

Martial skills are the same as any learning: they are a matter of personal ability and integrity. The dedication it takes to write poems or recite scripture is the same dedication it takes to be martial. Those who follow Tao understand that the value of being martial is not aggression toward others, but the development of skill, confidence, loyalty, and righteousness. The sword in the word *wu* is not to slay others, but to subdue the self.

Conflict

Song. *Conflict, contention, litigation.* On the left is the character for "speech." On the right is a phonetic for "public," "common," "general," "open," "justice," "fair," "equitable," "male," "duke," "lord." In this part of the word, the lines on each side represent division, and the line and circle they enclose represent something private; public is that which is brought out in the open for all. When there is argument over what is fair, conflict results.

   As long as one is in the world, conflict is inevitable.

Conflict is inevitable. We should take that as a given. We can try all we want to create utopian relationships, but conflict will eventually arise. People attracted to the pacifistic teachings of Tao sometimes fail to see that conflict has also been studied since ancient times. We who follow Tao make use of whatever comes our way—and that includes conflict.

   Conflict is an inevitable part of relationships—even an enemy is someone in a relationship with you. Therefore, all relationships are open to positioning and timing, and that inevitably implies strategy. The first rule of those who follow the Tao of strategy is to expose as little as possible. The second rule is to preserve life. The third rule is not to let go—for simply to break things off before the right time is clumsy and loses the benefit of the relationship.

   If the force of the other is too great, then deflect it, but do not surrender your intention and do not let go. Come back, just as the bamboo comes back after it has been pressed by the wind. If your opponent pushes you far, be prepared to go just a little further still, so that your opponent is exhausted. Then reassert yourself in the correct measure.

Strategy

Bing. *Strategy, war, military, soldier.* This is a picture of two hands holding a battle-ax.

The essence of strategy is to know when and how to apply force.

It is not that those who follow Tao never use force. It is just that they use force at the right time and the right place.

It is not that those of Tao never enter into conflict. But they do so as a last resort.

It is not that those of Tao never seek triumph. It is just that they know winning has its costs.

Therefore, at all times, those of Tao are aware of position and timing. If necessary, they act. If action is unnecessary, they remain obscure. Even for the most skilled person, winning can only be accomplished nine times out of ten. Therefore, the superior person is prudent and enters into conflict only when it is unavoidable.

In situations of life and death, one must bear in mind five elements: Tao, time, place, wisdom, skill. As long we manipulate these with understanding, we will win. If we neglect them, we will fail. In venturing out, seek natural advantages. If conditions are unfavorable, retreat. If you are faced with ten gates, leave one open for escape, but leave no opening for the opponent's escape.

Those who follow Tao know that conflict is inevitable, but that does not lessen its evil. Therefore, act if you must. If you must act, then act to win. But always prefer to live in peace.

Behind

Hou. *Behind, after.* On the left is the sign for "to step" or "to march." In the top right quadrant is the word for "fine thread." The bottom right quadrant means "to go." One walks, and a thread trails behind.

The follower of Tao dares not lead, but always follows.

The strategists say: "I dare not lead, but always follow."

They also say: "I dare not play the host, but would rather play the guest."

From these sayings, we see that the ancients studied circumstances before they set out. In situations of conflict, they preferred that their adversaries commit themselves before they took action.

We must make a careful distinction here: one should not be passive. One who merely waits is one who is too slow. Like a person who tries to sing while counting beats, if you wait for your cue to come, you have already missed it. You sing well only by knowing the beat and singing along with it. So if we apply the principle of "behind" correctly, it means that wise persons are skilled at anticipating their opponents' movements and blending with these actions. That is why those who follow Tao do not play the host but instead play the guest.

If you understand and master all this, then you can fulfill another famous saying: "I start out after my opponent, but arrive before he does."

Hard

 Ying. *Hard, obstinate.* On the left is the character for "rock." On the right is a phonetic character.

Those who follow Tao differentiate between hard and soft and know how to use them.

The masters continually talk about hard and soft.

Hardness refers to force, stiffness, tenseness, and the use of strength. Softness refers to yielding, touching, barely deflecting an incoming force, and remaining relaxed. Some make the mistake of emphasizing one over the other. The wise person knows that both are needed. One employs hardness or softness according to the situation, and often these two alternate with one another in less time than the blink of an eye.

Sometimes we have to be firm. For example, it is difficult to work with others unless one is clear about one's position. This is hardness, as in a hard edge along the contours of a highly defined drawing. At the same time, prudent persons know when to change if their position becomes untenable. This is softness—giving way to an opposing force in order to emerge unscathed.

With softness, we have sensitivity. With hardness, we can make assertions. It takes considerable practice and experience to understand these principles of hardness and softness, but the mastery of this simple duality can lead to great utilization.

Insubstantial

Xu. *Insubstantial, empty, vacant, deceptive, humble, weak, unprejudiced.* The upper portion of the word is a phonetic, and the lower portion of the word is extrapolated from part of another word meaning "none."

To be pliant is to have flexibility in one's very substance. It does not mean weak.

The bamboo, which gives way, survives a storm, while a brittle oak may be uprooted. Why? By giving way, the bamboo no longer occupies the space it did an instant before. It knows how to be insubstantial and therefore does not receive the full force of the storm.

By giving way, bamboo survives. It isn't diminished when it does this. With its strong roots, it doesn't lose ground. When the wind ceases to blow, the bamboo springs back to where it was. Indeed, the bamboo is quite a vigorous plant: It is long-lived, and evergreen, even in winter. It will not fall under the weight of the heaviest snows, because it offers no large limbs for the snow to settle upon. It seems to adapt quickly to new environments and grows back stronger after being subjected to the winter storms or the woodsman's ax. And its insides? Inside, it is empty. Those who follow Tao admire bamboo because it demonstrates how emptiness, vacancy, hollowness, and insubstantiality are quite vital.

In the adversity of life's storms, we should bend, but we need not break, and we need not give way. We should sink our roots down to the very wellsprings of life, nourish ourselves on the energy of heaven and earth. And we should look inside ourselves and understand just how emptiness functions inside of us. If we could learn the secret of *xu*, we would be most powerful indeed.

Round

Yuan. *Round.* Around the outside is the sign for "enclosure." Inside is a phonetic that also means "round." This is shown by a repetition of the outside square, thereby emphasizing roundness again, combined with a picture of a cowrie shell as an object that is round.

Those who follow Tao make use of the straight and the round.

Usually, it is said that the person of Tao prefers the round over the straight. Why do they say this? Since Tao moves in cycles, so too the person of Tao moves in circles. Because round is the shape of life—the fruit, the womb—so too the person of Tao loves roundness. Because a circle is eternal, so too the person of Tao cultivates the energy-conserving nature of roundness. Because returning is regeneration, so too the person of Tao uses roundness to generate new efforts. Because the circle has a center, so too the person of Tao gives orientation to movements. Because the circle redirects, so too a person of Tao saves him- or herself by deflecting all attacks into a circular motion.

But it would be wrong to think that the person of Tao never acts in a straight fashion either. The target must be shot. Two points must be joined. The one must be divided in half. A tangent must be drawn from the circle.

Those who follow Tao do not limit themselves to mere conception. Wise persons utilize the secret of the circle when it is appropriate, and they utilize the power of the straight when that is appropriate. They change when it suits the situation. This is why they cannot be opposed.

And in the constant changing, they show their understanding of the round.

Aggressive

 Lang. *Aggressive, cruel, wolf.* On the left is the character for "dog." On the right is a phonetic that means "good" and "sagacious." The wolf is considered aggressive but also very wise, as it knows how to escape danger and seek its prey.

If one is a hermit, one can be quiescent. If one is in the world, one must be aggressive.

To be aggressive, as the word *lang* shows us, is to have the prowess and cunning of the wolf. A wolf is shrewd. It does not blindly go into a situation. It scouts things out. It has a sense of itself and its surroundings that is nearly supernatural. Trackers have a hard time trapping it. Prey have a difficult time eluding it.

The wolf has its own "virtue" or moral force. It acts according to its own fixed rules. It does not kill excessively, it keeps to its territory, and it follows its instinct when mating and caring for its young. If only human beings could be so consistently true to their inner nature!

If those who follow Tao act on a worldly stage, they take the wolf as a model. They know that success in a situation is frequently a matter of aggressiveness. They do not waste their time in trivialities. Instead, they remain supernaturally aware of themselves and their territory. They track others, but in turn obscure themselves. And when the moment of action comes, they act without hesitation.

To be aggressive is the secret of success.

Stance

Bu. *Stance, step.* This is a picture of two steps of a person.

Without a strong stance, all other movements are impossible.

When ancient warriors trained, they laid considerable emphasis upon stance. Their practices were grueling. A beginner had to practice for hours, standing in low lunges, moving in all directions while carrying heavy weights, squatting for long periods on narrow wooden stakes, and moving strongly through the surging surf. The warriors insisted that one couldn't punch, kick, or throw a person without being able to maintain one's balance and plant one's feet firmly on the ground.

For those who follow Tao, having a strong stance is essential both physically and spiritually. The example of the stance can be applied to every situation in life: you always have to have—and know—your position. Don't be caught unawares. Don't be caught without a point of view. Don't be caught without tactics. The exercise of the stance teaches us that stance must be firm, but never static. From the insight and awareness of one's strategy, there are dozens of positions to which one can move instantaneously.

In life, as in the practice of stances, one must have both firmness and mobility.

Hero

Ying. *Hero, heroic, brave.* Above is the character for "grass." Below is a phonetic. This word originally indicated the highest tip of a stalk of grass, which was not only the tallest part, but the part from which the plant continued to grow. Later, the word was borrowed to mean "heroic."

Be heroic, but be smart too.

Why do we have heroes? Because it is part of what is most noble in the human heart.

Life is difficult to confront. Chance and ruin are overwhelming; the heart and mind are fragile. Those who manage to assert their will against the odds are admirable. When we are the ones who are able to triumph over adversity, we have reached a rare and fleeting moment.

No one can set out to be a hero. No one can fake being a hero. Being a hero is a matter of being prepared for a gift in time. Time will give you the opening. It is how you then respond that will decide whether you have taken advantage of your opportunity.

Having any less than heroic aspirations is to settle for mediocrity, and the mediocre never develop the perceptions and reflexes needed to follow Tao. But if you want to be extraordinary, concentrate only on perfecting yourself. Don't think about being a hero. In actuality, the degree of a person's heroism is often decided afterward. We needn't care about how others judge us. As long as we grasp the importance of a moment, meet the opportunity, and respond to it with the whole of our being, then we can consider ourselves heroes. This, then, is the true meaning of heroism: you met whatever came your way with every bit of yourself.

Life is simple, Tao is hard. By being heroic in life, we can make a beginning in Tao.

Means

Fa. *Means, laws, rules, model, arts.* On the left is the sign for "water." The rest of the word combines the signs for "deer" with the verb "go." A herd of deer followed its leader in escaping from danger. The leader would jump across ravines and even over water to escape (in the *Yi Jing,* water symbolizes danger). The other deer would see the leader's techniques for escape—his *fa*—and therefore find safety. The word *fa* is used in many compounds. The Chinese terms for a Buddhist teacher, a sorcerer, a judge, a lawyer, and numerous other judicial and spiritual terms all contain the word *fa.*

To go though life well is to have means at one's disposal. To have means is to know the laws of life.

How well will a person do in a situation? People ask, "How many *fa* does he have?" That is to say, the person who is the most resourceful is considered superior.

Legends tell of the Monkey King, a monkey with supernatural powers. In his exploits, he protects a pious monk who makes a long pilgrimage to India for Buddhist scriptures. Along the way, the Monkey King must fight the many different demons who wish to destroy the innocent pilgrim. The Monkey King even gets into a full-scale battle with the armies of heaven. He wins because he is cunning and creative: he has at his disposal seventy-two transformations, while the demons on earth and the generals in heaven are more limited in their abilities. They cannot match the Monkey King's large number of *fa.*

Coping with life is no different. Like the Monkey King, we must have many transformations. Whenever things are not going our way, that is a signal to change. This is called the live way. Those who cannot change, who remain fixed in stubbornness eventually lose. That is called the dead way. Demons and heavenly generals have their limitations. Those who follow Tao seek the means that transcend limitations.

Transform

Hua. *Transformation, change, metamorphosis.* On the left is a person with—on the right—an unfinished weapon. The weapon is in the process of being made; transformation is therefore implied.

Those who follow Tao avoid fixed movements and do not hesitate to act in unorthodox ways.

Tao changes very quickly. Life's circumstances shift so suddenly that they leave you breathless. Bitter feelings can arise in seconds. Great serenity can just as easily come in a moment. Life changes, and we must be just as quick to change too.

Those who follow Tao do not always do things the straightforward and orthodox way. Instead of acting according to preconceived ideas, they look for the greatest advantages. Structured thinking or clinging to prevailing dogma are only inhibitions. When following Tao requires reflexive action, inhibitions must be discarded.

When things go badly, those who follow Tao seek the causes and correct them. If the problem cannot be corrected, they shift the entire frame of reference so that the relative importance of the problem is diminished or eliminated. For example, if a general finds that weather and terrain suddenly become unfavorable, it is wise to change and lead the armies away, no matter how much the king wants battle.

Therefore, the wise solely follow the shifting and changing of Tao and avoid fixed routines. They do not stick stubbornly to ideas or patterns. Tao is formless, constantly creative, and relentlessly in flux. Those who follow Tao seek to change with it.

Leader

Jiang. *Leader, military general, to take, to hold.* On the left is a weapon. On the right is a hand holding meat. When the leader returns victorious from battle, he or she performs offerings and sacrifices.

The leader holds the organization together.

The quality of the leader determines
The quality of the organization.
A leader who lacks intelligence, virtue, and experience
Cannot hope for success.

In any conflict
The circumstances affect the outcome.
Good leaders can succeed in adverse conditions,
Bad leaders can lose in favorable conditions.
Therefore, good leaders constantly strive to perfect themselves,
Lest their shortcomings mar their endeavors.

When all other factors are equal,
It is the character of the leader that determines the outcome.

Near

 Jin. *Near.* On the left is the character for "movement." On the right is an ax. The warrior keeps his battle-ax close to him when going into battle.

The ability to judge distance is often the critical factor.

In the word *jin,* the warrior holds the ax close to himself as he ventures into battle. He knows his strength and is prepared to use it. If we could each master this simple awareness, it would change our lives completely.

The inexperienced overreach: they do not know their abilities and limitations. The veterans know exactly what is possible, and they keep everything they need close at hand.

The good warrior never blocks. Fighters in the theater make a big show of blocking and taking blows. But fighters on the battlefield fight close to their opponents and are efficient with their actions.

Among the ancients, there were duels between masters to show ability. In order to enhance the test of skill they often fought under special conditions. One such condition was to duel while standing on a set of overturned teacups on a four-foot-square table. To step off a cup was to lose. To fall of the table was complete disgrace.

The two fighters would jump up without any preliminaries. Their stances were so sure that they stepped from cup to cup with no confusion. All the while, they were punching, dodging, and even kicking during rapid shifts in their positions. Significantly, the duels usually ended in a draw—for great mastery was needed even to enter this tiny arena.

Can you imagine the ability to judge closeness these two masters had? They did not have to jump aside to avoid a strike; they simply twisted and turned at the last second while using that movement to launch their counterattack. A miss by a hair's breadth was good enough, for the closeness of the attack also allowed the closeness of the counter. This is something special to keep in mind when one is facing the battles of life.

Advantage

Yi. *Advantage, profit.* On the bottom is a dish, above is water. A ceramic dish overflows in abundance. (In business, activity "flows out." What is left in the dish is the profit.)

One who knows how to take advantage of natural forces will always be sustained. One who is ignorant of natural forces will be destroyed.

Those who follow Tao are extremely canny. They know the slightest details of what happens around them. Then they take advantage of them. Their lives appear miraculous, but all they do is take advantage of natural events.

There once was a strategist who was advising a general. Their side was greatly outnumbered, and they did not have enough arrows with which to fight. The general told the strategist that the battle was to occur in three days, and he feared that they could neither win nor escape. "Don't worry," the strategist said. "Leave it to me."

For two days, the strategist did nothing. The other side made menacing threats as they were clearly preparing for battle. The general was greatly worried, but the strategist merely entertained himself in his tent, calmly eating, drinking wine, and reading books. Finally, on the night before the battle, he ordered his men to put bales of hay into boats, light them with torches, and send them down the river that divided the two armies. He ordered his men to beat drums and make a great deal of noise.

The sleeping enemy was startled, and they furiously shot many arrows at the strange boats.

The next day, the strategist had enough arrows, and his enemy was exhausted.

In the same way, those who follow Tao understand hard and soft, upper and lower, inner and outer, cold and hot. They manipulate the balance of these forces in the ways that are open to them and protect themselves when events are unfavorable. Once they form their strategy, they can preserve their energy, because they know Tao. Because of this, they cannot be opposed.

Timely

Qia. *Timely.* On the left is the sign for "heart." On the right is a phonetic, the character for "union," and "harmony"—the triangular formation signifies the joining of two sides.

Timing is everything in Tao. To act in a way that is harmonious to circumstances and in accord with one's own heart is rare but precious.

In action, timing is everything.

> Force doesn't matter.
> Weight doesn't matter.
> Even being morally right doesn't matter.
> All that matters is timing.

The character *qia* reminds us that correct timing is something that must be felt in one's own heart. If a ballplayer tries to hit a ball and misses, it is incorrect to blame the ball. It is the player who is at fault. In the same way, those who would act according to Tao cannot blame Tao if things do not go their way. It is the individual who must discern what the time calls for and then act accordingly.

Timing means harmonious union. Clumsily destroying things cannot be called good action. To bring things together at precisely the right moment is what deserves to be called timing. A photographer captures light at the right moment. A bridge builder joins girders in correct succession. An investor buys and sells when the market is right. A fisherman throws the net according to the season and time of day. In these and all other professions, force, cleverness, determination, and power are meaningless if timing does not bring the right elements to bear. What matters is the right action at the right time.

Encounter

Zao. *To encounter, to meet, turn of events.* On the left is the symbol for "walking" and a path. In the upper right quadrant are two judges, represented by the double use of the character for the east (judges sat in the eastern halls). The character at the bottom represents their words of judgment. The right side means "magistrates," and it also means "many people." Along one's path, one encounters judges (or magistrates, or many people).

During encounters, the wise are careful to avoid confrontation.

If Tao is the flow of life, it stands to reason that this flow has a pattern. In some schools of Tao, this premise is interpreted literally. These schools create detailed calendars showing which days are good for certain endeavors and which days are bad. They show how land formations mirror the energy channels of Tao and teach that there are places of great energy as well as places of great danger. Each of us can probably think of times where nothing went right or when we entered a place that filled us with feelings of dread. The Taoists would say this was all due to Tao and the way it flowed or did not flow during certain times and through certain places.

Whether you subscribe to this type of Tao or not, it is useful to follow these Taoists' simplest advice: if you know the time is bad, avoid the situation. If you know a place is bad, avoid it. Evil is inevitable. But it is often possible simply to get out of the way. Some heroes advocate meeting things openly, fighting it out man to man, meeting force with force. Followers of Tao disagree. Whenever possible, they avoid bad times and bad places. They avoid confrontations. In this way, they make as many of their encounters as positive as possible.

Bold

Kan. *Bold, to venture, daring, audacious.* On the left is a picture of a bear. On the right is a hand with a stick. It takes daring to hit a bear.

You cannot go through life without being brave.

Eventually, the time of action must come. When that happens, be a winner. Don't settle for a mediocre result. Don't try to stay even. Go for it all.

With the intense training it takes to understand Tao, it is hard to get to the point of acting without any insecurity. The teachers criticize endlessly, the mistakes are numerous, and the high standards of skill are virtually unattainable. In addition, there is very little support for following Tao in this day. People would rather go for the easy life, and they ridicule those who try to perfect themselves. So it's hard to go out there and act like a winner. But that is exactly what you have to do.

Think of yourself in the midst of a challenge. What else do you have but who you are? You can't cheat, you can't prepare anymore, you can't look for help. It's only you. It is absolutely useless to permit self-doubt to enter into your mind. You may not be completely ready, you may not be certain if luck will be on your side, but nothing you can do will add to the situation. Just be your best and act like a winner and you will do the right thing.

You must still employ the five elements of strategy: Tao, time, place, wisdom, and skill. But in nine situations out of ten, life and death are determined in the minds of the contestants. Therefore, those who follow Tao know that the mind is supreme, and when putting themselves to the test, they know that boldness can be the deciding factor.

Lever

Gan. *Lever, shaft, pole, club, rod.* The character for "wood" is on the left. On the right is a phonetic. This is a relatively modern word.

The person who holds the right lever can move the world.

In ancient times, people had to erect levees and build canals to protect themselves from flood. It often happened that great pieces of stone had to be moved. Young people tried to apply themselves to the task, but the boulders were too big. Then the ancients showed them how to increase their strength just by the use of a simple rod.

Following Tao means to apply the principles of Tao. A lever is a good example. The natural laws that make leverage possible are there for anyone to use. They are universal; they are inherent. One needs no special understanding or "magic" to use a lever. One needs only the simple understanding of length, angle, and fulcrum. If one doesn't succeed on the first try, experimentation will quickly teach the proper approach.

Often people marvel at the abilities of those who follow Tao. But these abilities are nothing more than the knowledge of how to use the right leverage. Those who follow Tao are perhaps a little more observant than others, and they know when to wait for conditions to ripen before they act. When they apply the right amount of leverage, everything falls into place. For this, they are called miraculous. In actuality, any could achieve the same results—if only they knew the same principles.

Before

Qian. *Before, forward, toward, to advance.* The top part of the word shows a leg. On the bottom is a picture of a boat. When traveling up a large river, like the Yangzi River, boatmen sometimes had to get on the banks and pull the boat upstream by large ropes. In so doing, they had to go in advance of the boat.

To act in advance means moving forward when the time comes.

The time to act is not the moment of acting.
The time to plan is not when fate is upon you.
Those who succeed do so because they have already acted.
Those who fail do so because they act too late.

The people who are most successful have laid the foundations for their actions well in advance of the actual moment of challenge. Athletes have already done their training, so competition is a forgone conclusion. Painters have done their studies, so the painting is a mere formality. Attorneys perform painstaking research, so the trial is simply the performance of their strategy. In each of these cases, success comes from excellent preparation.

Those who follow Tao spend their lives building their character, testing themselves, training themselves. The methods those of Tao use to discipline themselves are more strenuous than the average life situation. Those who follow Tao employ these methods because they seek to accumulate a personal force to make themselves great. Then, when the moment comes to act, the power of their personality is overwhelming. In the vastness of their private discipline, they have already made themselves greater than those who do not follow Tao.

Daily situations require actions that cannot be met by trying or searching for answers on the spot. They simply require action. A true follower of Tao is simply the embodiment of artful action. Such people don't strain. They simply are.

Sparing

Xi. *Sparing, frugal, economical, to regard, to love.* On the left is the character for "heart" or "mind." On the right is a phonetic.

To be sparing is the way to traverse Tao without causing problems.

Everything we do provokes a reaction. It may be from others; it may be within ourselves; it may be as subtle as a small ripple in Tao itself. But there is no doubt about it: everything we do provokes a reaction.

The practice of following Tao is, in part, a way to minimize those reactions. In a sense, you are only acting as a "shadow" of Tao. By harmonizing with it, you blend with its momentum and any consequences are subsumed in the overall movement of Tao. This is called acting without acting.

However, this is not always possible. Then persons of Tao are very cautious. If there is going to be reaction, then they seek to use it—by deflecting it further, they dissipate the energy away from themselves or even harness it to yield an extra dividend. This is called the distant echoing the near.

The actions of those who have attained the mystery of Tao become even more intriguing. They have little or no consciousness of their own. They are so tied into Tao that what they do is completely as Tao would do. Such people have so opened their minds to Tao that they are not acting. Tao is acting. This is called emptiness within emptiness.

In whatever you do, be sparing. At the very least, you will avoid excess.

Multitude

Gao. *Multitude*. On the top is the word for "high," and it is a phonetic. Below is the word for growing grain.

Sometimes there is safety in numbers. Sometimes one must leave the multitude.

A hunter knows when to use the trees to cover his or her movements. One who follows Tao knows when to take refuge in a multitude.

A buyer knows that the price of something widely used will be lower than a rare item. One who follows Tao knows when to benefit from the multitude.

A chess master knows to hide the powerful pieces behind the pawns. One who follows Tao knows how to hide in the multitude.

But the hunter must catch the prey. The buyer must get the goods. The chess player must attack the opposing king. So too the follower of Tao knows when to emerge from the multitude.

The attitude is no different when it comes to spiritual matters. Why should we do something just because a certain charismatic religious leader says so? Again, those who follow Tao take part in organized spiritual activities when they are still learning. However, they should never give up who they are or their determination to know Tao. Tao is higher than any religious leader, and each of us should strive not to be more devoted to an institution, but to be more devoted to the universal Tao.

Part Five

MOVEMENT

Dawn

Dan. *Dawn, morning, daylight*. This word shows the sun above the horizon.

In the beginning was darkness, and the first ray of light represented the first movement.

At night, the ancients gathered their families and students around them and often did nothing else except withdraw into contemplation. Just as the plants, the sun, the earth, and the waters all quieted into the darkness, so too the masters willingly became part of the night. Night, they explained, was what life was like in the very beginning. There was no world. There were no phenomena. There was only darkness and stillness.

In the early morning, the ancients opened their eyes from their meditations and awoke the younger ones who had not the discipline to bear witness to the entire night. The masters gently pointed to the dawn: the lesson of life's beginning was repeated daily. The world began when the first ray of light flashed across the darkness. In the same way, morning, and the entire world, begins when the first ray of dawn illuminates the night sky.

Therefore, if we want to know about Tao, we need only remember that we are part of a way constantly dawning.

Flow

Xing. *To march, to walk, pathway, flow, business.* This is a very old word and was derived from an aerial view of crossroads. Since the crossroads are the coming together of so many people and ventures, the image was eventually extended to numerous meanings. This word can simply mean "walking." It can mean "movement." It can also mean a business—banks, for example, are called "Silver *Xing,*" or the Silver Business. In philosophy, the most fundamental elements, the Five Elements, are called the Five *Xing.* So *xing* means something both fundamental and dynamic.

The fundamentals of life are neither static nor mechanical; they are dynamic.

The sun traverses the sky, the rivers flow on, the seasons come and go as steadily as the revolving of a wheel. Everything is part of the great and eternally moving Tao.

The ancients studied the phases of the sun, but they did not ask what the sun was made of. They contemplated the river, but they did not scoop up the water, imprisoning it in a bowl, to see why it moved. They accepted the seasons, but they never considered whether time could be stopped. Instead of isolating things and breaking them down, they were content to observe how these changes took place and concentrated on how people could fit in with that relentless movement.

The ancients felt that life had to be considered in its entirety and that separating it into different categories was an intellectual effort that could not ultimately help the understanding of Tao. For example, if someone wanted to know how a human body worked, the ancients suggested studying the body as it lived and worked and functioned. They found dissection of limited use: How could a cut-up corpse answer a question regarding life? Life was to be understood by inquiry into the living. Life was to be understood as an eternally changing process.

Tao is not material, it is dynamic. If you want to know it, study its living movement—its *xing.*

Change

 Yi. *Change, easy.* This is a picture of a swiftly moving lizard, the image of change.

Those who follow Tao spend a lifetime studying change.

The ancients observed that all life changed. Grain grew from seeds to tall, full plants. Deer were born in the spring and gradually learned to walk on their own. Human beings grew old, and died, and yet the generations succeeded one another.

Observing the continual alteration of birth and death, the ancients therefore said Tao had no fixed points: its only constant is change.

When something reaches its extreme, it changes to its opposite. Just after a rice plant reaches a sweet fullness, it begins to yellow, wither, and die. Just as the deer comes to full vitality, it soon becomes old and passes from the earth. And when people reach the apex of their knowledge and strength, they inevitably begin to decline.

Thus it is that Tao is movement, and that movement is marked by constant change.

Return

Fan. *To return, to turn back, to turn over, to rebel, polarity, opposites.* Two hands are held opposite one another.

One needs to understand cycles to understand Tao.

Days and nights, summers and winters
Waves curling up, consumed by new waves,
The ongoing march of generations,
The vapor of water congealing into clouds—
Tao is cyclical, not linear.

The multitude of things are innumerable,
But they travel circularly.
Those who accord with Tao
Understand rise and fall
And gain clarity and insight.
Those who do not accept rise and fall,
Ride recklessly with misfortune.

Thus it is said: the secret of Tao lies in returning.

Adapting

 Sui. *To adapt, to follow, to accompany.* The symbol in the center represents "movement." Divided on each side is a phonetic composed of the signs for "wall," on the left, with "left hand," and "body" on the right.

The ability to adapt can mean the difference between success and failure.

The crux of following Tao is to know acceptance. If you want to go east, but Tao wants you to go west, then you should go west. If you want to accomplish ten things, but circumstances only allow you to accomplish nine, then accept that. If you meet obstacles to what you want to do, you have to ask yourself how you can adapt. Sometimes you will be able to overcome the obstacles. At other times, you will have to go around the obstacles.

In ancient times, armies in nearly every culture fought in formation. They used phalanxes, troops, squads. Commanders loved to sweep from the left, then sweep from the right. They set up their archers in orderly rows and had them fire in regulated sequences. But what happened when these orderly forces met "disorderly" guerrilla warriors? They frequently lost. Ambush, night attacks, unorthodox tactics, violation of rules, infiltration of ranks, exploitation of terrain and weather—all these approaches, at one time or another, overpowered well-disciplined, well-equipped, and well-organized armies. Why? Because one side adapted, while the other side did not.

The same is true of the individual. One should never be too proud to adapt. If you see that things are not going your way, adapt quickly. By doing it in a smooth and timely manner, you can avoid disrupting the flow of events. This is called Tao.

Drifting

 Liu. *To drift, to flow.* The three lines on the left side indicate water. The top part of the right side shows a waterfall; below, a river flows away from it.

If we trust in Tao, then life flows for us. If we follow Tao as we follow a stream, then life is easy.

The students constantly asked the ancients, "How can we be happy?" And the masters laughed, not so much because of the question, but because the worry and seriousness of the question put the students even further from their goals. The ancients were fond of saying nothing was needed to follow Tao. One master even went so far as to say he was a boat, adrift on the water, floating here, floating there, without any concerns at all. Life was his boat, and Tao the river.

It is a challenge to accept the constant flux of life, but the greater challenge is learning to ride that flux. Different people have different preferences as to how to do this. Some want to go through life literally drifting, as the master's words imply. But as is often the case, what the masters of Tao say and what they do are quite different! The masters say they want to drift here and there, but in reality, they frequently engage in arts, strategy, and positioning. It's a fine point indeed: we may be floating on Tao, but there is nothing wrong with steering.

If Tao is like a river, it is certainly good to know where the rocks are. We also need to know the swiftness of the current. Then when going downstream, we can utilize the river's full force. Willy-nilly drifting will not lead us unharmed down the center of the channel. That is why there is the study of Tao. That study is our rudder in the tremendous current of Tao.

Travel

Yu. *To travel, to float, to swim, to rove.* On the left is the character for "water." On the right is a phonetic. Some forms of the word show this part of the word as a flag—when the wind blows, the flag moves. When combined with the symbol for water, we have a double idea of movement and, by extension, travel.

To travel means to trust Tao.

Whatever you want to know of life you can learn by traveling. Whatever you want to know of people you can see by being with them. Whatever you want to know of nature is best known by being in nature. Whatever you want to know of Tao you can know by floating.

As one floats on water, so too are we all sustained by Tao. As a swimmer must understand the current, so too will we learn about Tao by traveling in it.

Tao has direction.

Tao has consciousness and no consciousness.

Tao has unlimited creativity.

Tao is life, and death, and that which is neither.

Tao is mighty.

Tao is mystery.

Tao is supreme.

Tao is universal.

Tao is everywhere.

There is nothing that is not Tao. It is only that human beings imagine themselves separate from it. That is like a swimmer going out into the waters without checking the conditions. If she refuses to acknowledge the waters, she will be destroyed. But the swimmer who floats and moves according to the currents is not only sustained, but enriched.

All you need to do is to trust in Tao and travel in Tao and all knowledge will be yours.

Movement

 Dong. *To move, to excite, to begin.* On the left side is a phonetic and the word for "heavy"; the top part shows a person squatting down, perhaps to lift something. The right side is the word for "strength"— someone is exerting great force to try to move what's heavy; by extension, then, "movement."

In order to be sensitive to Tao, one must be able to discern its motion.

How good is your sense of Tao? Can you feel the earth's rotation beneath you? When you seek the great center, can you sink to the core of the earth?

Even as we travel through life, we have to keep to our own center. The constant and great movement of Tao can be overwhelming if we do not know ourselves. It is essential to learn about our inner selves as we learn about the outer Tao. Only by keeping to our hearts can we have the equilibrium needed to face the immensity of Tao.

Even when we meditate, an activity that seems very still, we have to sense the dynamic power of Tao, for all living beings move. Even when they are still, their hearts and minds continue to act. So the stillness of meditation doesn't truly mean that there is no movement. It is just that the madness of the human mind is stilled, so that we can sense the more subtle—and true—movements that are always happening around us. That is the paradoxical way to find movement—through stillness.

Be still and feel the movement of the earth, and the center will no longer be a question.

Star

Xing. *star*. Three stars are shown above. Below is a phonetic.
    We should fix ourselves on the bright.

All too often, our lives remain in the darkness of ignorance. We flounder around, and that only perpetuates our sorrows.

In the night sky, the stars always make us wonder. As children and as adults, we never tire of looking at that sparkle. Storytellers of old attributed meaning to the constellations. Strategists foretold the future by their movements. Sailors on the sea navigated by them. For centuries, the stars have inspired both wonder and direction.

In our lives, we must all navigate. We must choose our course and walk our path well. The stars in our lives are our goals. Without goals, we are lost. It is important to take the long-range view of things. Where do we want to end up? That is one star. What do we want out of our study of Tao? That is another. What do we want to accomplish in our lives? That is another. What work can we do that will be the most fulfilling? That is yet another star. In this way, the wise person creates a personal constellation and navigates unerringly by it.

That is why those who follow Tao are considered incredible. Actually, they have simply picked where they are going and are making their way toward those goals. To others, who are lost in the vastness of Tao, that seems unusual: when the crowd is confused, then the person of determination becomes superior. But in actuality, such power is open to any who would use it.

Direction

Xiang. *Direction, to face, to favor.* This is a picture of a small north window under the eaves of a house. When one looks out a window, one is looking in a particular direction.

If we would only return to our natural selves, our direction would be unerring.

Why is it, in all the wide blue sky, the bird knows which way to fly?

Perhaps it looks at the ground for reference points. Maybe it can only go forward, following its beak. It could be an inner dictate of its mind. Or perhaps it's instinct.

The ancients said that the bird follows Tao, since it is a natural creature, unsullied by human conceptions.

For direction, look to nature. For direction, look into yourself—is it not possible that we have within us an instinct for direction as strong as the bird's? If you can find that—and it most assuredly exists in each of us—then Tao is sure to follow.

Road

Lu. *Road, way, type of something.* The left side is the character for "foot"; it also means "enough," "full," and "pure." On the right is a phonetic.

No one can walk a road for us. We must each walk ourselves.

Everything we do in life forms a road. Our life span, our aging, our career, our endeavors, our relationships—all of these form a sequence that becomes the road we walk.

When we walk along a road, we should not regret another road not taken. Those who are mature accept this. We cannot travel on one path while walking another. If we go to one destination, then it is inevitable that we will miss others.

It is tempting to linger upon regrets and suppositions, especially when times are unhappy. Maybe we could have been more famous or richer. Maybe we could have done more as we grew older. But it is far better to remember that we make our own road one day at a time. If we have been fully involved with our own lives and have been making our own decisions, there is no reason for regret.

As we grow older, it becomes critical to fulfill what we find important. The more we understand our goals, the more we can properly gauge how close we are to them. That gives us a very powerful understanding.

The road each of us walks is our own personal Tao. All the principles we use in following universal Tao are also applicable to our personal one. Just as there is only one great Tao, so too is there only one Tao for us—our Tao. To be true to that, to be sure in that, is never to be separated from the essence of wisdom.

Stele

Bei. *Stele, stone tablet, memorial stone, tombstone.* The character for "stone" is on the left. On the right is a phonetic that originally meant "ordinary" or "humble."

We should encourage ourselves by recognizing the markers along our path.

When all we have to walk is the lifelong way, we need some sense of where we are and how far we have gone. We need some sense if others have been this way before. We need to know when we are leaving one stage and entering another.

This is not always easy. It is not always perfect. But it is important to note certain milestones:

When you think of others before yourself, that is Tao.

When you discipline yourself, that is Tao.

When you feel an activity doing itself rather than your doing it, that is Tao.

When you are aware of what to do spontaneously, that is Tao.

When you can take responsibility for what you do, that is Tao.

When you cultivate different skills with complete attention, that is Tao.

When you enter into lucid stillness, that is Tao.

When you are better than your worries, that is Tao.

When you can control your health, that is Tao.

When you can combine mind and action, that is Tao.

When you can be like water, that is Tao.

When you can be as illuminating as fire, that is Tao.

When you can be as sharp as metal, that is Tao.

When you can be as piercing as wood, that is Tao.

When you can be as abundant as the earth, that is Tao.

And when you can make yourself like a rock at will, that is Tao.

Run

Zou. *To run, to travel, to go, to hasten, to depart.*
Above is a person, below the sign for "foot."
  Since Tao is a path, the only possible act is to travel it.

Tao moves, and you must run to keep up with it.

If you do nothing, nothing will happen to you. If you wait for a god to grant you a reward, you will wait futilely. If you want entrance into an institution and a fancy initiation to bring you success, you will be disappointed. To follow Tao means that you have to go out and be a part of Tao. The road will not be traveled without your actually running along it.

When you experience the road, then whether you make a mistake or not, you have the opportunity for learning. If you miss the potential lessons, that is the fault of inattention, not of being on the road. Whenever you act, something happens. And whatever that something is, it contains a potential lesson.

Don't like what happens to you? Then change. But do something. When you change, something else will happen instead. There is no such thing as no response. A response will always come. It's just up to you to figure out its meaning.

That's how immediate Tao is. But you have to do to meet it. The word *zou* reminds us of what we should do. This is a person: you, traveling the ancient way.

Broad

 Guang. *Broad, enlarged, large hall.* The strokes covering the top and left symbolize a house, but since only one side is shown (the other is so far away it is out of sight), the idea of immensity is implied. Inside is the phonetic meaning "yellow"; it is composed of the signs for "light" and "field." The idea of a large shelter and the vast earth are thus combined to signify "broad."

Tao is a path. The land through which it passes is broad.

Tao is a path. Tao is the way. But what is Tao like?

Is it like a breathtaking landscape painting in which the figures are dwarfed by mountains and streams?

Is it like walking in the wilderness, isolated from all people by thousands of miles of uncharted territory?

Is it like exploring a deep and dark series of caverns, to be lost in a place that smothers light, sound, and time?

Is it like sailing the oceans, afloat on the powerful and constantly heaving surface, with no place for reference or landing?

Is it like flying through the air, with nothing to impede the flow of sky and clouds and wind?

Being in Tao is like all of these images and more. Tao is vast, Tao is broad, Tao is eternal. But how can you put a name on something infinite? How can you say that Tao can be contained in a few thousand words—or even all the words ever written? None of these efforts can come even close to defining Tao. Gauging and categorizing the infinite only result in more infinity.

A person can know Tao, because part of every human being has the potential to be infinite too. Infinity can know infinity because the two are actually a single broad unity without end or beginning.

Complete

Jiu. *To complete a cycle, to go, to follow, to make the best of, immediate.* On the left is the word for "capitol," which originally meant "high," "elevated." On the right is a phonetic showing a right hand above a person. A person is jumping up high in order to complete a task.

Only after many completions of cycles can there be wisdom.

Tao moves in cycles. The ancients declared that when an event reaches its zenith, it descends toward its nadir. When a phenomenon reaches its extreme, it changes toward its opposite. Everything moves in cycles.

Those people who watch dynasties wax and wane know this. Those who watch the natural cycles know this fact all too well—the turning of the planets, movements of the oceans, the extremes of the weather, even the buildup of stresses resulting in earthquakes are phenomena moving on cyclical paths.

Even the most minute events of our lives move cyclically. Our successes and failures, our family relationships, our finances, our participation in groups—all these things move in circles. The way of Tao is to note and take advantage of these rhythms. This requires extensive experience over a long period of time. You may have disappointments and blunders along the way, but there is no other better method of learning.

Just remember to see your cycles through to completion, as the word *jiu* implies. It is important not just to move in Tao, but to complete the cycles in order to learn. We cannot know the circumference of a circle until we have completed at least one revolution.

Part Six

SKILL

Art

 Shu. *Art, skill, magic.* This is a combination of the word *xing*, meaning "flowing" and "ventures" (derived from an image of crossroads; see p. 79), with the word for growing grain (in the center). If people want to harvest grain, they must know the art of growing.

Knowing the steps to create living growth: that is art.

The ancients sensed the enormity of Tao and wanted to accord with its rhythms. They saw Tao in everything they did, for any endeavor in life generated its own way—a *tao*—and any endeavor was made better by having the knowledge to do it. Thus the ancients strongly emphasized skill. Tao was not to be followed passively. It was to be used, with artfulness.

Those who followed Tao in ancient times often had the reputation of being magicians. They could heal people through herbs and massage. They could predict the coming of rain. They could direct the building of waterways and walls. They could farm with great efficiency. They could craft items of daily need out of ordinarily available materials. They could defend themselves against animal and human predators. They could travel without fear. They could read the most abstruse writings. They could converse with anyone, from the highest emperor to the simplest laborer. All these skills and more the people declared to be miraculous.

But did the ancients possess some mystical secret? They did not. They only appeared to be magical, because they had skills others did not have. Given the opportunity, anyone can learn what they knew. Just as the ancients tried to master many arts so they could then follow Tao fearlessly throughout the world, we too should continue to pursue our learning and inner growth. Then, no matter what situation arises, we will have the art to face it.

Divination

Bu. *Soothsayer, to divine.* This word represents the veins on a tortoise shell. In early times, soothsayers conducted divination by heating a tortoise shell. The way the shell cracked formed primitive ideograms, and the soothsayer would divine the message from those words.

Those who follow Tao are their own instrument of divination.

In olden times, people sensed the greatness of the universe and tried to live in harmony with that magnificence. In order to communicate with the unseen, they tried the medium of tortoise shells. They heated the shells over a fire and when the shells cracked, they looked there for the words they needed. Frequently the words were esoteric, and so a soothsayer of great learning, experience, and purity interpreted the words.

In later times, there were spirit mediums. Special oracles—men and women who were virgins, who never ventured into the world to be polluted by its contradictions, who never tasted of animal flesh, who kept themselves pure through meditation, who were venerated by those who protected them, who maintained their insight through constant studies of the classics—allowed themselves to be the conduit between the human world and the divine. The gods would speak through their mouths or use their hands to write words in trays of sand.

Today, we must become our own soothsayers. Why? To depend on tortoise shells or oracles is still to have distance between us and Tao. We want to feel Tao directly, realize it within us. We must be as skillful and pure as the diviners in the past, taking inspiration from the high standards of personal purity they maintained. We must reach Tao for the sake of our own understanding. Nothing rivals a direct link to Tao.

Tap

Pu. *To tap*. This is a picture of a hand (the lower part of the word) holding a diviner's rod.

To act is the way to touch Tao.

Whenever a person of Tao wanted to commune with the gods, he or she would set up an altar. On this table, made from the best and heaviest woods, were placed the various instruments of offering: trays of fruit, candles, sacred books, a jade scepter, wine for purification, a peachwood sword, a writing brush and different colored inks, special handmade paper on which sacred words were to be written. Then the person would perform rituals, special dances, prescribed steps, and esoteric body postures. Only then could the implements be employed and intercourse with the divine accomplished.

That was how Tao was practiced by people in the past. Perhaps this seems superstitious and mad. But taken on the metaphorical level, we can still learn much from it. To approach Tao, we must do it seriously and with great concentration. What is important is not that we have ritual objects, but that we *act* in order to engage Tao. Tao comes to those who seek it. Like the hand holding the stick in the word *pu,* we must reach out.

Dance

Wu. *To dance, sword fencing, posture.* This is a picture of a dancer. The triangle at the top is a hat, the decorations below are feathers held in each hand, and below are the two feet.

When you dance, you move with Tao.

Dance is part of the very origins of Tao. When the ancients wanted to understand the movement of Tao, they danced. When the ancients tried to utilize Tao, they danced.

The shamans danced to bring rain. Priests danced in constellation patterns to call the gods. Meditators danced between their sittings for exercise and health. Mediums danced to invite spirits into their bodies. Exorcists danced to control ghosts. Warriors danced to demonstrate their exploits and to hand down their techniques. Storytellers danced to bring history alive. Dancers danced for beauty.

You cannot think about dance. You cannot count the beats or tell yourself to do this step and that step. Instead, you have to act in a way that puts aside your everyday conscious mind. You just have to dance. You can't make it look any better than what it is, and if you are honest, you can't make it any worse: you can't hide yourself when you dance.

If you dance and you give yourself over to the movements, then you will know exactly what Tao feels like.

Medicine

Yao. *Medicine.* The two cross shapes at the top are the sign for grass and plants—most medicine was herbal. The word below is the word for both "joy" and "music" and is used here phonetically (see p. 100). The best medicine maintains balance and harmony.

In ancient times people's bodies were susceptible to the pernicious influences of the weather and the consequences of overwork. Emotionally, they suffered the difficulties of a feudal society. Naturally, the ancients sought to heal the sick, but they also preached the more preventive methods of maintaining health. For them, true health meant complete balance and harmony, between body, mind, and spirit, and with Tao.

Through experimentation, collaboration, and observations of animals, the ancients developed their medical knowledge. Since they believed that balance and harmony were at the core of all healing, they sought herbs—which came from the world of nature—to bring people back into balance not only within themselves but with the world around them. Later, methods of massage, osteopathy, exercise, acupuncture, and surgery were added to their repertoire—but the aim was still the same: to keep a person in balance and harmony.

Since most people were ignorant of health and hygiene, the ancients did not keep their knowledge a secret, but devoted themselves to teaching and healing. Their tradition of compassion is still important. First, those who follow Tao try to help those they meet, whether the needs are medical or otherwise. Second, those who follow Tao always seek balance and harmony within themselves—harmony of self must be the basis for bringing harmony to others. Thus, medicine is the art of equilibrium. Although some doctors prefer to deal with extreme illnesses, those who follow Tao would rather make immediate and subtle adjustments.

If you are on the road of Tao and you need healing, seek out the means to acquire it. Whether that means going to a doctor or learning how to maintain your own health, it is a vital part of following Tao. And if you have achieved balance and meet someone you can help, never turn away. Skill is to be used not just for yourself, but for the good of those you meet. That, too, is balance and harmony.

Recite

 Nian. *To recite, to read, to chant, to consider, thought, reflection, recollection, memory.* Below is the character for "heart." Above is the character for "to be present." This is shown by the triangle that symbolizes union coupled with a hand touching someone (indicating contact). Recitation makes knowledge present in the mind ("heart" and "mind" are considered synonymous).

The purpose of recitation is to make knowledge so ingrained that the true human can come out.

In the ancient academies, students recited for hours each day until poetry became part of their minds.

In the opera schools, performers practiced choreography and singing until the arias emerged spontaneously.

In the studios, painters practiced strokes day and night for fifty years, so that a single image of a flower would fool a bee into landing on it.

In the temples, the worshipers chanted holy scriptures until they became absorbed into Tao.

In all these cases, the purpose was to absorb knowledge so thoroughly that it was "forgotten." It became a part of the person, as natural as blinking the eyes or breathing. In modern times, many people balk at repetition in the belief that it blocks creative expression. But those who follow Tao still feel that repetition is important in the acquisition of skill. It is not a means of subduing the individual but of uplifting the individual. Only after the issue of technique is addressed can the true person emerge.

Long cultivation is necessary in order to practice Tao skillfully. But eventually, all methods are absorbed. Then technique falls away, leaving the true person—present at his or her most human.

Music

Yue. *Music, joy.* The top shows silk strings stretched across a wooden frame, representing a *guzheng* (Chinese zither). Some interpret the center part showing a circle with a horizontal line as representing the mouth of a singer. In either case, music is being played, and this makes both the performers and the audience joyous.

The music of nature is entirely different from the music of the academy.

There was once a zither student whose master, frustrated by his pupil's lack of musical progress for so many years, pronounced him unsuitable for learning. To understand how devastating this was to the young man, one must remember that playing the zither was considered a very high and demanding art, practiced only by refined and learned people. In addition, one's master was like a parent. He or she was usually as dedicated to teaching as a parent is to rearing a child. So to be rejected by his teacher was a great shock to the student.

The master abandoned the young man on the shores of an island, leaving the student only a zither. Left to his own resources, the disappointed pupil provided first for his survival. The island, although uninhabited, had enough wild fruit and vegetables to sustain him. In the time that followed, he listened to the singing of birds, the chorus of the waves, the melodies of the wind. He spent long periods of time in meditation and musical practice. By the time he was rescued, several years later, he had become a virtuoso player and composer, far greater than his master: he had entered into Tao.

And so it is with us. We need teaching. But there is a point beyond which teaching cannot provide for us. Only direct experience can give us the final dimensions we need. That means learning from nature, and learning from ourselves. As long as we remember that, there can be no mistake.

Ability

 Neng. *Ability, talent, skill, energetic.* This is a picture of a large bear—the head is at the upper left, the body is on the lower left, and the paws are on the right. The bear possesses great vitality and so became a symbol for "ability."

To possess ability is to be self-reliant.

Tao is a person walking along a path. No one is carrying that person. There is no vehicle pictured. Following Tao is something each of us must do by ourselves.

But the path is difficult. It will test you. Walking in the mountains is hard enough. Rain and snow fall on you. Storms wash away the mountainside. Earthquakes shake the ground. Steepness wears at your legs. In life, the spiritual path is even more difficult. Although everything you want out of life is on that path, there are people who will hinder you and situations that will oppress you.

What do you do when life is difficult? You could call for help, but that is not always reliable. Sooner or later, life will catch you with no one around.

You might be without food or shelter during a time of natural disaster. You might be alone at a time when help cannot come quickly enough. You may even suffer the tragedy of having all your friends abandon you. That is why those who follow Tao emphasize the importance of having many abilities. If you have the self-reliance that comes with having many skills, you will not lose your equanimity. This cannot be emphasized enough. You cannot truly walk the whole path of Tao until you can cope with any unknown.

People say that those who follow Tao are serene, but that serenity is not because of some meditative trancelike state. It comes from the confidence of one who has ability.

Eat

Shi. *To eat, food, cooked rice.* In the center is a square with a horizontal line representing cooked rice. Below it are lines representing aroma. The rice is fragrant and entices people to eat it. Above is a phonetic.

Without controlling how we eat, we cannot control our existence.

Cooking rice is a fundamental act. A few scoops of grain are put in the pot. Clean water is added to the rice. The water, which turns cloudy from the leftovers of the milling process, is then poured off. The washing is repeated until the water runs clear. Then the pot of rice is slowly boiled over living fire.

Let us consider for a moment. What you get in life is earned—rice doesn't come to you in a dream. You have to work to get it. Every grain is therefore precious. That's why we try not to lose any during washing or waste any when we're done eating. It is no exaggeration to say that those who follow Tao have a personal relationship with how they eat and with what they eat. Only then do they have a chance of controlling their destiny.

Going back to cooking rice, we have to be careful that the water is hot enough to cook the rice, but not so hot that the pot boils over. When the rice is cooked, it can be ladled out carefully. Cooking rice is a simple task that we do over and over again, practicing it with mindfulness. Maybe enlightenment will one day occur before the pot is done boiling.

Practice

 Lian. *To practice, training, experience, piece of silk.*
On the left is the character for "silk." On the right is a
phonetic. Practice means repetition, like a piece of silk
that is repeatedly dipped into dye.

To practice is to organize oneself down to the very
fiber.

In order to obtain silk, silkworm cocoons must be boiled before
the thread can be pulled out. It takes many more hours of dyeing
and weaving to make finished cloth. Perhaps that is why the idea
of practice is equated with the refining involved in the process of
making silk. Beginning students are raw, like the thread that comes
from the silkworm. Only after the refinement of practice can they
become like precious finished silk.

When the students went to the ancients to learn Tao, the masters therefore emphasized the word *lian,* "practice." As long as the
student practiced, then understanding of Tao was possible. There
was no restriction based on gender. There was no requirement
that one come from a certain class. There was no stipulation that
one have some mysterious talent. Young and old, rich and poor,
any were welcome to follow Tao. But they had to make the effort.
They had to purify themselves of bad habits and misconceptions.
They had to work to acquire skill, so that they could not only help
others, but live their lives in independence. That took a long time.
It took practice.

The more you harmonize with Tao, the more easily you can go
back to it. The more you apply the lessons of Tao to your daily situation, the more skillful you become in moving through the intricacies of life. All this is elevated by practice. Like a woman reeling
silk, those who follow Tao constantly draw themselves into finer
and finer levels of meaning.

Spear

Qiang. *Spear.* The word for "wood" is on the left, and on the right is the word for "granary." The right half of the word probably has a purely phonetic function, although it is easy to see someone with a long staff guarding a storehouse.

The true tip of the spear is not the weapon, but the user's ability.

Ancient warriors emphasized the importance of fighting without weapons as well as with them. For them, the skill of the practitioner came first. So they drilled over and over in the basics of body movement, stance, and response.

This went on for years and years. They had to train constantly, because they lived or died according to their abilities. When they went to the battlefield to fight aggressors, to defend emperor and homeland, they did not hide behind foot soldiers. They did not engage in treachery. They relied only on their own skill. They were people of honor, courage, and self-reliance.

The warriors repeatedly told each other the story of a fighter famous for his prowess with a spear. As long as anyone could remember, he had never lost a battle. His enemies tried to catch him unawares, but he always had his spear and was able to defeat them. Finally, one day when he was drinking at a well, his opponents caught him without his spear.

He died in the battle because he could not fight without his weapon. In spite of his fame, he still had not mastered the art of fighting. In the same way, we can utilize anything we want in life, as long as we remember that the truest techniques come not from things, but from ourselves.

Collect

Zong. *To collect, to bundle, to sum up, to unite, to comprise, to manage.* The character for "silk" is on the left. On the right is a phonetic, the word for "excited," "alarm," "restlessness," represented by combining the symbols for "window" and "heart": when one is excited or restless, one looks out the window in anticipation.

Those who follow Tao cultivate many arts, but they bundle them together with the subtlety of silken thread.

In the cultivation of different arts, it is tempting to run them together, to come up with some unprecedented synthesis. That is fine if you are looking for new forms of artistic expression, but it is not necessary for following Tao.

Those who follow Tao may have wide-ranging interests, but they will pursue each of them within its own confines. For example, a person who practices both calligraphy and music will strive to gain mastery in each area, but she won't necessarily worry about mixing the two.

In the same way, there is nothing wrong with studying other spiritual systems. But if you enter into another spiritual system, then do things strictly within that tradition until you master it. That is the way to excellence. If you try to apply Tao to another tradition before you understand it, you denigrate both that tradition and Tao.

However, once you progress to a high level in each, there is nothing wrong with practicing both. You don't need to do anything consciously. They will combine in your life spontaneously.

You cannot make two sticks into one stick, but you can tie them together with the silken thread of your understanding.

Secret

 Mi. *Secret, private, divine.* The left side is the sign for spiritual influence. The right side shows a weapon hidden beneath the two halves of a robe.

What is most precious is always kept secret.

There was a man who had seen divinity. He wrote down his experience carefully, and then sewed the papers into the lining of his coat. It was not until he died that someone noticed the odd bulge in the lining and people discovered his talisman.

Do you think this man ever had doubts about what he had experienced?

And isn't it significant that he understood that it had to be kept private?

The true sage has no doubts about revelation and needs no one else to confirm it.

Market

Shi. *Market, marketplace.* This is a picture of a banner hanging from a bamboo pole. Vendors with stalls in an outdoor marketplace used to hang out a sign.
Tao's value is personal, not commercial.

People use whatever they can to make money. If they have invented a fabulous device, they market it. If they have suffered misfortunes, they sell their story to the curious. Family problems, murder, adulterous affairs, sexual perversions, and far worse all become moments for greed, not shame.

Will the strategies of Tao help us do well in stock investments? Will an understanding of human nature allow us to gain a competitive edge? Will athletic development allow us to strike a more impressive profile in a crowd?

Those who try to use spiritual learning for glory will always be disappointed. It doesn't work that way. Learning about Tao is for the sake of being a better person, not for being a wealthier person. Somehow, the knowledge works in such a way as to thwart profit-making motivations.

The ignorant see no way to profit by Tao and so they do not value it. That's all right. Tao is there for those who can see it. It is there for those who hear it. It is there for those who need it. For all others, it is as invisible as the wind that blows the banners in the marketplace.

Jin. *All, exhausted, completely, entirely, end.* At the bottom is an elevated dish or vessel. Above it, a hand is shown with a lid to the vessel. Nothing more is to be put in, so the task is complete and at an end.

Always complete your actions.

When you do something, don't hold back. Shoot it all, go for it all. Don't wait for a "better time," because the better times are built on what you do today. Don't be selfish with your skills, because the skills of tomorrow are built upon the performances of today.

It's so tempting to say, "I'll keep it for myself and build it up to something really big later." Only later never comes. By waiting too long, the end catches up with you. You will then be "covered," like the lid in *Jin,* and you will never have had the chance to act.

To be with Tao is to live a creative life. To live a creative life always means that you express who you are. And expression is never helped by suppression. Expression always benefits from coming out. Then more inspiration will come from that source.

When you act, act completely. Follow through. Do everything that has to be done. Be like the fire that burns completely clean: only from that pure stage can you then take the next step.

Part Seven

CRAFT

Work

I Gong. *Work, skill, a good job.* This word is derived from the word for "heaven" (see p. 5). In ancient times, the emperor was called the "son of heaven." Everyone else on earth existed to work for him. Therefore, removing the character for "person" (see p. 201)—the emperor—from the character for "heaven" left the word "work."

To live is to work.

When we work, we learn. There is something boring about someone who has never done anything with book learning. Indeed, that person's knowledge is quite limited. We learn much more by doing. Testing oneself against the limitations of material, time, and skill is critical to self-development.

It is important to do the type of work that leads not simply to production, but to skill. In other words, the most important type of work is the kind that results from one's life, not from societal or economic pressures. When we work as part of life it leaves a profound residue in our personality. It produces an attitude of accomplishment, an accumulation of working wisdom impossible to obtain any other way.

The ancients recognized this phenomenon so clearly that work came to signify skill. The kind of work one does—farm work, art work, spiritual work, or any other work—is not so important. What is important is that one performs one's work at its most profound level. In olden times, people would say that a craftsperson who had achieved great skill had realized the Tao of that art form.

And once one has realized Tao in part, the whole is not far away.

Artisan

Jiang. *Artisan, craftsperson.* The large C-shaped part enclosing the whole word represents hollowed out wood. Inside is an adze in the process of scooping out the wood. An artisan is a skilled person who can wield a tool.

Craft takes spirit and produces spirit.

Does a tool have a spirit of its own?

One of the rules that the ancients taught about tools was that no one but their owner should touch them. A tool had a spirit and should only be handled by its owner.

For many centuries, craftspeople valued their tools, building elaborate toolboxes as virtual shrines to their precious tools. Then, with industrialization and the conversion to factories, owners pushed for greater efficiency and mass production. They eliminated personal tools and required workers to check out implements from a central crib and return them after use. Pride in tools and personal standards of craft were destroyed.

Some people scoff at these attitudes. To them, the belief that a tool has spirit is plain superstitious. "An object is an object," they say, "nothing more and nothing less."

But that attitude overlooks the opportunity to use craft as a means of self-realization. A spirit may be no more in a tool than in a temple, but the fact remains that respect for that spirit creates a tremendous change in the artisan. By respecting the spirit in the tool, the artisan really focuses on his or her own perception and skill. The true spirit in the tool is nothing less than the artisan's pursuit of perfection.

Angle

Jiao. *Angle, corner, animal horn.* The horns are on top, and the remainder of the word represents the body of an animal.

What it takes to hold an angle is worth considering.

You can build a table simply by resting a plank of wood on two upright slabs, like the stones at Stonehenge. But where those stones have stood for centuries by their sheer weight, three pieces of wood poorly placed on top of one another would not stand well.

The ancients therefore worked according to traditional forms. Their tables lasted, not because refined principles of engineering were understood, but because they arrived at certain forms empirically. These forms became both construction and aesthetic standards simultaneously.

We eat at tables. We worship at tables. There are few endeavors for which we do not need a table at some point in the process. It is the table that has helped lift us above the level of brutes. It's good to build tables, to understand this most basic of structures, and to endow this most fundamental of furnishings with our aspirations. The importance of fixing the angles of a table therefore has important ramifications.

To put two things together and then hold them at the proper angle is one of the miracles of skill. That is true for more than just making tables. Nothing in life can be useful if we do not first support it, set a level place from which to work, and then secure those angles with knowledge, skill, and experience.

Lasting

Jiu. *Lasting, long period of time.* This is a picture of a person with his or her way impeded (shown by the stroke on the upper left). It takes a long time to overcome impediments; this represents the idea of a long time.

Work for what is lasting.

It is more trouble to go for what is lasting. People want immediate results and often do not consider the future. The problem is that mere expediency will invariably come back to haunt you. The cheap and fast solution becomes useless after a few years and you then have to start over again. Perhaps, over the course of a lifetime of replacement, you even spend more time, effort, and money than if you had acquired or made a lasting item to begin with.

And what of the time spent? Let's say you need a chest. It is far better to buy one or have a craftsman make you a good one—and then never have to waste time on the issue again—than it is to live out of a series of bags, cardboard boxes, or flimsy wooden ones.

And what of what you do in life? It is far better to do a quality job each and every time in whatever you do. Whether you are repairing a broken door or paying attention to your meditation, do the very best job you can. Then your problems will be fewer.

As you work for what is lasting in life, you build on everything you do. You go that much further with the quality that builds up. But if you waste your energies on trivialities, then neither you nor your accomplishments will be lasting.

Sharp

Guai. *Sharp, rapid, prompt, quick, happy, satisfied.*
On the left is the word for "heart." On the right is a
picture of a hand (on the lower right) holding an object that has just been divided in half. Splitting is instantaneous when force is applied, but quickness
depends on the mind, and so the word for "heart" is
also present (heart and mind are synonymous).

Sharpness depends on the edge of a blade narrow-
ing to nothingness.

A master carpenter once said that he had reduced the number of
his tools, and those that were left were all he needed for the rest of
his life. He never let anyone else use them, and he never used anyone else's tools. All of his implements fit into a single box. Working as a builder of temples and tea houses, he cut and planed all
his joints by hand.

The master worked seven days a week. Out of those seven days,
he spent fully half the time sharpening his tools, until the backs of
the blades and the bevels of the blades met at angles so perfect that
the edges narrowed to nothingness. In this way, the master worked
with the edge of nonexistence.

Those who prefer expediency say that all this is a waste of time.
We should just use a power saw, hack the piece of wood in half,
bolt or nail the parts together, perhaps with a reinforcing angle of
iron, and be done with it. It's a waste of time to spend half of one's
energy doing something that doesn't even show in the final work.

But of course it does show. It shows in the beauty of the temple.
It shows in the master, for when the master is sharpening, he is
already building. When he is honing his blade, he is making his
mind keen. In fact, his way of working is very fast, for by the time
he has the wood in his hand, the cutting of the joints is a mere formality, and they fall away as simply as fruit falling from the tree.

Hand

Shou. *Hand, handy, skill, workman.* This is a picture of a palm.

That which is made by hand improves both the maker and the user.

In the recent past, everything was made by hand.

The objects that were made did not have the precision and regularity of machine-made things. In turn, however, the objects had spirit.

Even today, "made by hand" carries a certain attraction. We associate this phrase with quality, care, and artistry. When we have objects like this, we feel a personal affinity with them: someone made it with great attention, and we cherish it with attention.

Those who make something by hand feel enriched by doing so. They are working on something tangible, something that can potentially outlive them. They have the opportunity to make things their way, to put all the work necessary into them, to do things because they feel it is right, not just because it may be cost-effective or marketable.

Over the years, their hands take on a wisdom of their own. The potter knows by touch when something is out of round. The furniture maker knows by feel when something is straight. We who follow Tao therefore value what the hand does. We want a personal relationship with what we do and how we live: there is no better measure of this than the breadth of one's hand.

Proficient

 Shou. *Proficient, experienced, ripe, cooked, intimate.*
This is a picture of a hand (on the right) roasting lamb
until it is cooked thoroughly.

The longer one practices, the more proficient one
becomes.

Proficiency is no longer held as an ideal today. In
the past, craftspeople took pride in their work. Today, too many
things are done for the sake of money and not for the sake of
human beings.

Therefore, it is not surprising that people complain that following Tao is too complicated. They would rather be told that there
is nothing to be done. But after years, such people still lament the
difficulties of their lives. If they would invest the time trying to
strive for perfection in at least one area of life, they would realize
rewards far greater than their initial accomplishments. There may
very well be too many classical books, too many techniques to
master, too many philosophies to remember. But if one actually
begins on the path to learning instead of yearning for the easy way
out, it actually gets easier after many years.

When that happens for you, it will seem as if the more you
work, the less needs to be done. You will check. Have you forgotten something? But you will see that you have not. What you
labored so hard to perfect is now tossed off without a second
thought. That is the sign that work truly has become a part of you.
You have reached the level of proficiency.

That is why the masters say: "The more I work, the less I know."

Combine

Lien. *To combine, to connect.* On the left is the symbol for "ear." On the right is a phonetic, a picture of silk on a loom that symbolizes union.

    The correct approach to life is to pay attention—and harmonize—both sides of every issue.

If you are weight lifting, it is good to do pulling movements as well as pushing movements.

If you are a musician, it is good to sing the notes as well as play them on your instrument.

If you are an artist, sketching is as valuable as painting.

If you are a boxer, dodging has as much tactical usefulness as striking.

If you are a doctor, diagnosis is as critical as treatment.

If you are introspective, it is still beneficial to spend time with others.

If you are extroverted, it is still helpful to spend time alone.

Those who follow Tao understand that combining methods, rather than isolating them, yields the greatest results. It is not that we will never specialize. But whatever discipline we enter, we must make sure to survey the whole of it. Each technique we learn will then fit into the next one, until we amass a contiguous set of methods. By combining, we compound learning to extraordinary dimensions.

Finish

Wan. *Finished, complete, done.* Above is a picture of a roof, representing a house. Inside is a phonetic. To be finished is to put a roof overhead.
Complete every endeavor.

Those who fritter away their energies are ineffective. Those who concentrate surpass others. If you can count the time you've wasted in a day, then you know how much room you have for improvement.

The remedy for this is very simple to state but highly difficult to accomplish: finish what you begin. That takes incredible concentration. Once you try this a few times, you will understand. First, you will become more realistic about what you can take on. Second, you will marshal all your skill and the greatest perseverance to go the distance. Third, you will be able to complete your task. Fourth, you can only progress by building on the distance you have come.

Finish what you start. That is the great rule when it comes to action. But when it comes to personal development, you are never finished. The great are supreme only because they understand this.

Do you want to know what Tao is? It is the distance you cover from start to finish. It is that simple.

Part Eight

CONDUCT

Young

Shao. *Young, few.* The top three strokes represent two halves divided by a central line, suggesting an object made smaller by division. The stroke at the bottom is yet an additional diminishment, so that the entire word means "the smallest of the small."

The young need guidance to attain wholeness.

Life is a daily process of compromise, murky meanings, and ambiguity. What is correct one day can be wrong the next. What seems good can all too easily become bad. For the old, many years of disappointment often produce a bitterness hard to dispel. It is not right to pass this feeling on to the young.

The ancients themselves had attained Tao and no longer acted according to fixed rules. With their decades of experience, they could act with subtlety and grace in the midst of life's contradictions. But they knew that the young could not act in this way. The ancients therefore gave the young clear rules and simple answers. Recognizing that young hearts longed to be good, the ancients taught rules of conduct that would last until a young person could understand the contradictions of life.

The young are pure, innocent, tender. The young need guidance. Simple and clear answers are necessary. Later, when the young have walked their Tao long in the world, they will transcend all rules.

Pine

Song. *Pine*. The left side is the symbol for "wood" (branches above, roots below). The right side is a phonetic and has several meanings. One meaning is "lord" or "gentleman," and certainly the pine was regarded as one of the grandest of trees. The other meanings for this word are "public," "open," "common," "fair," and "just."

The pine, the grand old man who stands in the open.

When the young needed guidance on the matter of character, the ancients were wise enough to show, not lecture. In response to questions about how a person should act in the world, the ancients took their students to the mountains and showed them a pine tree.

No matter what the weather, the pine tree stands in the open. Its nature is constant, its branches evergreen. When the rains pour down, the water runs off the needles, the drops lingering at their tips like shining diamonds. When flooding comes, the pine holds fast to the rock with its tenacious roots. When the sun bears down, its needles do not shrivel, but provide shade impartially to all who come to its shelter.

The ancients therefore urged their students to "stand like a pine." No matter what the travails of life, remain rooted loyally to family, friends, and ideals. In dealing with others, be unafraid of acting openly and honestly. And in the examination of character, be as constant as the pine is green—always.

Then, like the pine, we shall always grow toward heaven.

Loyalty

 Zhong. *Loyalty, honesty, sincerity, earnestness.*
Above is the word for "middle." Below is the word
for "heart"/"mind."

    An honest and sincere heart is one that cleaves to
the middle.

It is simple to espouse loyalty.

But how easy is it to be loyal?

There was once a great general who was leading his troops to
repel invaders from the north. He was on the verge of pushing
them back beyond the Great Wall. However, the prime minister
was his enemy. Taking advantage of the emperor's involvement
elsewhere, the official issued an imperial edict to recall the general.
Understanding that patriots along the way might intercept the
edict, he sent out twelve messengers, each with the edict and a
golden medallion. A single one of these medallions required complete obedience by the edict's recipient.

As the prime minister anticipated, loyal warriors moved to stop
the messengers. But one got through. When the general saw the
golden medallion and the edict to return, he stopped the attack
and mounted a horse for the capital. For days and nights, he traveled the hundreds of miles back. Along the way, ordinary people
and warriors alike begged him not to go: everyone knew of the
prime minister's evil. But the general refused. He had sworn always to obey the imperial edict.

Before the emperor could return, the prime minister imprisoned
the general and had him beheaded. To this day, this general represents the paragon of honesty and loyalty.

Can we be so loyal to our own determination to follow Tao?

Can we live by keeping our hearts centered, even in the midst of
danger?

Jade

Yu. *Jade*. This word was originally identical with the word for "emperor." It is a combination of "earth" (see p. 6), below, with a single horizontal line above representing the emperor. The emperor is he who rules over all the earth.

Jade might be shaped and polished, but it cannot be forced to be anything that is not according to its nature.

The purest jade is beautiful. It is constant, cool to the touch, with a surface that can be both hard and soft at once. For many centuries, jade has symbolized great human virtues of courage, intelligence, and purity.

In its smoothness was seen benevolence. In its possession of angularity without cutting sharpness was seen righteousness. In its "willingness" to hang down in beads or fall to the ground was seen humility. In its clear, bell-like sound when struck was seen music. In the fact that neither its beauty nor its flaws could be concealed was seen loyalty. In its radiance was seen faith. In its brightness was seen heaven.

Jade's purity cannot be compromised. You cannot adulterate it. You cannot hide its flaws or its beauty. Jade exists in its own right. Those who follow Tao emulate the qualities of jade and thereby attain uncompromising integrity.

Orchid

Lan. *Orchid*. Above is the sign for "plants." Below is a phonetic. Originally this word actually denoted the cymbidium, but it has since come to mean all sorts of orchids.

Both the orchid's beauty and fragrance pervade its environment without partiality.

Why is the orchid a symbol of love and perfection? It is not only beautiful and pure, but its fragrance will perfume a room without favoritism. It brings loveliness into our lives not out of effort, not for motives of profit, not after negotiations have been carried out and money exchanged, but simply out of its own exquisite character. For this reason, the orchid is the symbol of refinement and impartiality.

An orchid blooms slowly, living on the rarest of waters and the purest breaths of air. It buds delicately, languidly. An orchid cannot go to war. It cannot build bridges. It cannot fly though the air. And yet human beings, for all their cleverness and scheming, can neither duplicate its beauty nor manufacture its scent. Fake orchids are useless, just as it's useless to imitate refinement and friendship.

Thus those who follow Tao strive to be pure in character and impartial in love.

Bamboo

Zhu. *Bamboo*. The picture shows the stems and leaves of bamboo.

A poet wrote in the fourteenth century, "Bamboo: without mind, yet it sends thoughts soaring to the clouds."

Why is bamboo a symbol of exemplary conduct? Because it makes use of emptiness.

The insides of bamboo are hollow, but the plant can withstand wind and snow, and grow with great vigor. The ancients admired the bamboo's emptiness because it showed "no mind," that is, no egotism. Human beings' problems, the ancients felt, were caused by egotistic self-identification, an insistence to see people as separate and even superior to nature. A person of "no mind" would have no such self-identification, and would therefore be wholly integrated with the great natural order. Therefore, when discussing proper conduct, the ancients used the bamboo as an example: it was empty inside, and yet it was vigorous and long-lived.

The ancients also pointed to bamboo's many uses. Young shoots are delicious food. Pulp is used to make paper. Early books were written on strips of bamboo. Stems can be used for pipes, buckets, masts, furniture, scaffolding, fences, rafts, sculpture, and chopsticks. Leaves can be used for raincoats, thatch, and packing. Seeds are used for decoration. Leaves, sap, and roots can be used for medicine. The ancients lauded bamboo's many uses as an example of great generosity.

Finally, the bamboo is a great example of integrity. Node after node fit into each other. Leaves arch gracefully off the main trunk on bright green branches. Every part of the bamboo does its part in an orderly way. When challenged by storm, the entire plant bends, but does not give way. It sways, but it can seldom be broken.

The ancient lessons therefore urge us to emulate bamboo. In bamboo's hollowness, understand "no mind." In bamboo's versatile usefulness, understand generosity. In bamboo's flexibility, understand integrity.

Comb

Shu. *Comb.* The word for "wood" is on the left.
On the right is a phonetic.
    The comb both separates and unifies.

How strange a comb is. It enters the hair and separates the strands. But afterward, the hair falls together in an orderly mass.

How clever a comb is. When it is put into hair, it can stay there and hold the hair in place. Yet it does so without exerting itself. It borrows the strength of the hair.

How even a comb is. Its effectiveness is due to its regular and evenly spaced teeth. To be regular and know intervals—how worthy of emulation those qualities are.

How useful a comb is. Without it, we could not untangle our hair. Would that any of us could be so useful in sorting out the confusion of daily life.

How decisive a comb is. When wielded on its edge, it can part the hair with a swordlike absoluteness. If only we could learn to part the tangles of delusion with such surety.

How humble a comb is. It will lie in its owner's tray without complaint, happy to do its single function. In this way, it is modest and yet survives. Other implements are battered in their functions—hammers, knives, millstones are all worn down in their functions, but the comb undertakes no such labor and is preserved.

How gentle a comb is. It has teeth, and yet it does not bite. Could we be so careful with our strength?

How like a comb are persons of Tao. Such persons enter into the thick of entanglements and yet leave nothing behind. Such persons add nothing and take nothing away. Such persons leave nothing untouched and yet afterward leave no trace of their own.

Friend

You. *Friend*. The word shows two hands acting in the same direction.

We cannot be friends without trust.

Unless there is trust between friends, there can be no closeness. Once that trust is established, friends can unite to do things in common. Thus, the word for "friend" shows two people acting toward a single goal.

It is said that there are three levels of friendship. The first is the level of casual acquaintance. The second is where there is sharing. The third, considered most deep, is the level where we trust friends to criticize us. Ulterior motives at any one of these levels ruin people quickly, and we cannot call such relationships true friendship. When we are with a true friend, we will know, because we can be open and trusting. Such openness is friendship.

Cynics hold that we should look out for ourselves first. This may be superficially good, but ultimately it will impoverish us. Unless we have friends with whom we can share good times and bad, we will never know selflessness. And not to know the selfless trust of friendship is to miss an opportunity to understand our own best qualities.

Compassion

Ci. *Compassion.* At the base of the word is the symbol for "heart." The upper part is a phonetic.
If you have a heart, you have compassion.

When it comes to suffering injustice, there are two types of people. The first says, "I can't wait to turn around and do this to someone else." The second says, "This was done to me, and I do not want to do it to someone else."

When it comes to spiritual accomplishments, there are two types of people. The first says, "I will press on for myself because my knowledge was won so dearly." The second says, "I will help others, because I know how difficult it is to walk a spiritual path."

When it comes to facing death, there are two types of people. The first says, "My life is at an end, and I am bitter." The second says, "In sharing, I became more than myself and cannot die."

Lose

 Diao. *To lose, to fall.* On the right is the character for "hand." On the left is a phonetic.

To fall is inevitable. To learn from defeat is rare.

The first technique ancient warriors taught their students was not punching. It was not kicking. It was not even blocking. The first technique they taught was how to fall.

No matter how great the master is and how high the hopes for the student are, a great many defeats come before winning. It is foolish to assume that one will never be hurt or thrown during a fight. Therefore, it is wise to practice falling, so that you will be prepared and protected. Those who ignore this step may have courage and strength, but they will not survive.

There is much to learn from falling. If you would want to know how to tumble your opponent, it's good to know how it feels to be thrown. If you want to have a stable stance, it's good to understand instability. If you want to have balance, it's good to know just how far away the ground is. In fighting, as in spirituality, one learns about others by learning about oneself.

Even with the lessons of falling learned, it is still a long climb up the pinnacles of life. The higher you climb, the farther you have to fall. It's best to ask yourself how great your desire is—and like the hand in the word *diao,* how strong you are—before you boast about how far you will climb.

Correct

Zheng. *Correct, orthodox, proper, upright.* The topmost horizontal line is the limit. Below is the character for "foot." To be correct is to stop at the proper limit.

Although Tao is limitless, those who follow Tao know how to set their own limits.

Tao is infinite.

The world has a myriad of appearances and realities.

A human being's desires oftentimes have no end.

Given these three observations, what can we do?

We try to discern the patterns of life and harmonize with them. Although Tao is vast, we try not to let ourselves be washed away in its endless current. We look at the way Tao flows and travel in that direction.

In the face of the world's myriad opportunities, we try to discern what is advantageous to us and avoid the detrimental. We do not move in the world without discrimination, but try to use our own experiences—and not the unreliable opinions of others—to make choices. Thus, although the world is vast, we travel though it in increasingly wise ways.

Even though we acknowledge that our desires are great, we try to pare them down to their most essential. The way to do this is never suppression, but a constant and steady give-and-take between our energies and our opportunities. From the palette of desires with which we were born, those who are wise choose the wholesome. We also recognize that we may have unwholesome tendencies, and rather than feel guilty about them, we seek to discharge them harmlessly. We understand that the more twisted our upbringing and experiences, the more perverse our desires become, so we try to heal the scars of our younger years and keep our lives harmonious.

All this requires discipline, but discipline is the only way to cope with the overwhelming nature of life. The person who is disciplined always acts correctly. One who always acts impeccably is like the strokes in the word *zheng*. Everything is clear, and everything meets at right angles and in perfect proportions.

Righteousness

 Yi. *Righteousness, harmony.* The top part of the word is the character for "lamb." The bottom left shows the word for "grain" and represents a field or rice paddy. The bottom right shows a weapon; someone is protecting a rice paddy.

In trying to follow Tao, there will invariably be conflict between the ideals we pursue and the realities of our lives. Unless we accept this situation, and even learn to work with it, we cannot have the harmony of Tao.

While it's true that you must pursue truth with no thought of gain, you must, sadly enough, also pursue truth with little thought of support.

Among the ancients was an official well known for his sense of righteousness. He advised the emperor not to begin a war of aggression against a neighboring state, but the emperor listened to the warriors instead. In retribution for the righteous official's unpopular position, the emperor banished him to the wilderness.

The righteous man watched the kingdom fall to ruins in the fighting of the unjust war. Even from afar, he appealed to the court to stop its aggression, but the court rejected his petitions again and again. After some time, he could stand it no longer. He wrote a long and passionate poem. Then he drowned himself in a river. The people hurried to save him, but arrived too late. It is said that they even threw precious rice into the water in the hopes that the fish would not eat the body of this loyal poet.

Life remains as difficult for each of us as it was for this righteous man. We may have lofty ideals, but they are easily thwarted in this turbulent world. The ancients often said, "The more you try to live a good life, the more you will suffer." It's true. We must be receptive, even to misfortune: the depths of our character are only revealed upon trial.

Charity

 She. *Charity, to give alms, to bestow, to part with, to abandon.* On the left is the character for "hand." On the right is a phonetic.

One can only help others with an open hand.

Throughout the centuries, religions from all over the world have tried to persuade their followers to be generous. They promise all sorts of rewards if a devout person shows charity. But it is a fact that there is no special deal to be gotten by being generous. We should simply be kind because that is the right thing to do. We won't get a direct reward in exchange for our kindness, and yet nothing else can so awaken us to the spiritual within.

When first one considers others beside oneself, spirituality arrives. That has been the case with many holy people, both in the schools of Tao and outside of it as well. A famous prince begins to seek spiritual understanding after seeing the sorrow of illness. A rich woman seeks spiritual understanding after becoming aware of those poorer than she.

When a child first offers something to the parent, the parent knows that that child is developing awareness. When a person first puts the needs of a lover ahead of his own, he then begins to know love. It seems paradoxical, but there is no dispute: in selflessness lies the most direct way to understand the self.

If you recognize in others the same poverty you have felt, try to alleviate it. If you recognize in others the same hunger you have felt, try to feed them. If you recognize in others the same loneliness you have felt, try to cheer them. If you recognize in others the same discrimination you have felt, try to champion them.

It is when you recognize in others the same human condition you experience that you are on the verge of knowing yourself.

Kindness

Hui. *Kindness, benevolence, favor, charity.* Below is the character for "heart." Above is a phonetic.

The deepest kindness comes not from simply thinking of others, but in feeling what they feel.

We were all taught to do unto others as we would have them do unto us. That is fine, but there is still room for mistakes. True kindness comes not from those who just think of how it might feel to be hurt, but from those who actually *do* feel it. Can you feel hunger? Can you feel poverty? Can you feel homelessness? Can you feel disease? Can you feel injustice? Can you feel desperation?

If you felt any of this in your own life, you would surely do whatever was in your power to alleviate it. Similarly, if you meet others who are suffering and you have it within your power to help them, you will—if you can truly feel what they feel.

The masters lecture us over and over to be compassionate, so much so that even the least pious student would have to try. But just to *try* to be compassionate still makes it seem like an exercise or moral obligation. Those who are truly kind are so not because of theory or ethics, but because they feel the suffering of others as directly as they would their own.

That ability to feel human need can develop your sensitivity to feel Tao.

Virtue

De. *Virtue, moral excellence, power.* The left side symbolizes "movement." The right side is primarily of phonetic significance, yet its meaning can still be instructive. The top is the word for "upright," the middle shows an eye, and the bottom is the word for "heart."

When actions are upright and from the heart, we have moral excellence.

The virtue of Tao is frequently discussed in moralistic terms. People say, "We want to show that we believe in Tao, so we act in a virtuous manner." That is only a narrow, social definition.

Tao itself has power. And if we tap into that power, we not only attain its life-giving properties, we can also act from its pure source as well. It is futile merely to discuss the power of Tao; it has to be experienced.

Once Tao has been tapped, it changes a person. Tao is not just some intellectual idea to believe in, it is a state of being. When one touches Tao, one feels at one's most human. Existence seems to be at its most profound.

If one feels all that, then there need be no rationale for being a good person. One simply *is* a good person because that is the natural way of things. That is why the ancients did not emphasize the discussion of ethics and morality. Rhetorical exchanges could easily be distorted by argument and interpretation. Instead, they trusted in the transforming power of Tao.

Therefore, for those who follow Tao the questions of good and evil are moot. We know the right way to act because we take our cue from Tao.

This is just as the word for "virtue" reminds us—go out, be upright, and Tao will change your heart.

Part Nine

MODERATION

Center

Zhong. *Center, middle.* One interpretation says the word shows an object cut exactly in the middle. Another says that this is a target, with an arrow piercing the bull's-eye.

When we understand the importance of moderation, then we will automatically operate from the center.

In all matters, the ancients counseled moderation. For them, the primary sin was excess, for excess destroyed all sense of what was human and plunged a person far from a true way in life.

If all of life can be thought of as a continuous walk along a great path, the worst thing in life is to lose one's balance on that path. That is why the ancients continually underscored the need for moderation with the word *zhong*.

It is a clearly drawn word—a target with an arrow piercing its center. For the arrow to hit the target, it must fly true. If the archer inclines to the left or right, even by a mere fraction of a hair's breadth, the arrow will not fly a true path. And once an arrow has hit its target, it has attained the only correct spot—any other place shows imbalance.

So whenever we are confronted with the impossible in life, we need only think back to what the ancients would counsel: be moderate. If we keep that as our aim, then there will be few mistakes in life.

Pair

Dui. *Pair, opposites, parallel sentences or couplets on scrolls hung opposite one another, to face one another, to correspond with, to suit, to match, to agree.* On the right is the word for "inch" or "to measure" and represents the hand in general. On the left is a phonetic.

Opposites are really pairs. We cannot have one side without the other.

The ancients believed that all things are divided into opposites, and that it is the interrelationships of these opposites that cause all phenomena in the world.

We have a male side and a female side. We have a left and a right. There is up and down. Without opposites, we literally would not exist.

The trouble comes when we are unable to view things with moderation. We all want to be rich, but we don't want to be poor. We all want happiness, but we shun disappointment.

That is why the word *dui* is so important. It reminds us that opposites are not mutually exclusive but are actually pairs. If we have sadness, then happiness will come too. If we have love, we will also have to deal with conflict. For all our learning, we will have days where our philosophical outlook will be tried to its breaking point. For all the peace of meditation, we will still have to face work, illness, and stress. There is no path in life that only stands on one side of a pair and never ventures into the other. The sooner we accept—and work with that—the better off we will be.

That is why the way of Tao is the middle way. We cannot have one side without the other in life: it is wisdom to strike a balance between them both.

Happiness

 Fu. *Happiness.* The left side means a revelation from heaven and is used in all words with abstract meanings. The right side shows the word for "beans" on the top and "fields" on the bottom; when the beans are harvested, people are happy.

All abundance is provided by Tao. If we appreciate that, we will see that we are surrounded by happiness.

Like everything else in Tao, happiness comes from within. What minimal support we need from the outside—a bit of food, some shelter—can actually be very simple and plain and is readily available. Nevertheless, people are unhappy because they do not know moderation.

"All I need to be happy is to be rich," many say. But the newspapers are filled with stories of wealthy people who live in deep despair. In fact, the simple phrase, "All I need to be happy is to be rich"—complete with your choice of substitutes for the word *rich*—is an immediate indication of the source of our unhappiness: there is no end to what we want.

Know when enough is enough. Some die from hunger, but many die from overeating.

So to be happy, we have to control our desires. The ancients taught two ways to do this. Sometimes they used discipline to curb desire. Sometimes they satisfied their desires. This is the genius of Tao: moderation. We do not need to cleave to the extremism of the ascetic. We do not need to lose ourselves in the indulgence of the hedonist. We follow Tao, the middle path.

Longevity

Shou. *Longevity*. This is a combination of the word for "old" and a picture of a turtle shell (the tortoise lived long and thereby symbolized longevity). Another interpretation is that this word shows the pattern of furrows in a field.

Those who live long know the way of moderation.

When the ancients farmed, they carefully plowed the fields of the golden earth. They worked the land with simple tools, breaking up the earth to receive the seeds. They brought water from the ponds, where the turtles lived as witnesses to many human generations.

Year after year, the ancients plowed tirelessly. If they stopped their work, they would not only jeopardize their survival, but they would fall out of step with the seasons and thus with Tao. So they continued, and in the process of honest work and steady labor they emulated the turtles by acting slowly and methodically. Their lives grew long.

Generation after generation, we have worked the same fields. We continue to plow, we continue to make the rows of our furrows as even as possible. How regular the furrows are, how balanced they are. How they follow the contours of the earth. How they are plowed in order to take advantage of the sun and the rain. If we want the joy of longevity, we need only contemplate the balanced, proportional, and even plowing of fields.

The ancients taught that anyone who would like a long and healthy life must simply dwell in a good and clean manner close to the earth. Nature provides everything. Although we must work to gain any benefit, the sustenance is still there, awaiting our hand. It has always been so, since ancient times, and it will always be so.

To plow the field requires moderation. To plow the field requires discipline. To plow the field requires skill. As long as one exercises each of these things carefully and in the spirit of Tao, then longevity will be close at hand.

Hungry

 Ji. *Hungry, dearth.* The character for "food" is on the left. The word on the right is a contraction of the word for "few." Hunger comes when food is scarce. The follower of Tao stays hungry.

Those who follow Tao know hunger and scarcity. Thus, when times are difficult, they know how to survive. When times are rich, they remember to be cautious.

Those who follow Tao make great achievements, if they are so inclined to come out and act in the world. Nevertheless, they always stay hungry, so that they are never complacent. They are always out trying to do better. Like an immigrant eager to make a new life, or a boxer trying to win a title, or a tiger searching the jungle for its prey, those who follow Tao know that hunger is a great motivator.

In eating, be moderate. Leave a little room in your stomach. Try to stay lean, not for the sake of fashion, but for the sake of health and motivation. The mind grows sluggish on too much rich food and fine wine.

However, neither should one become a "hungry ghost," forever searching the world for something to eat. That is too much the other extreme. Like everything else in life, those who follow Tao use moderation, and they use everything they can—even hunger—to further their travel through Tao.

Full

Bao. *Full*. The left side means "to eat." On the right is a phonetic that shows an embryo inside a womb and, by extension, represents anything full.

Having enough to eat: that is joy. Knowing when one is full: that is wisdom.

If you don't want people to rebel, then stuff their bellies full of food. If you want no wars, then make sure there is enough to eat. When a country is on the brink of ruin, it is because the leaders have taken too much in taxes, conscription, and labor.

In a simple life, people eat plain food. They have enough. No one needs to lecture them about balance: nature teaches them. They grow their own food, they eat what comes into season, and they consume in proportion to their own labor. They learn to save some, they learn to share, and they learn that for everyone to have enough creates contentment.

Eat what is proper. Eat what is right. Although there are elaborate schools of cooking, avoid excess. Although there are fanatic beliefs about diet, fasting, and ritual, avoid obsession. Eat what is natural. Eat enough, but don't eat too much. The simple application of that dictum is difficult enough.

Passion

Qing. *Passion, love, emotion, affection, feeling.* On the left is the character for "heart": feeling is a matter of the heart. On the right is a phonetic and the sign for "purity," derived from an image of pure color (see p. 31)

Feeling and emotion are the colors emerging from the heart.

Not to have feeling is inhuman.
To be carried away by feeling is foolish.
Not to have desire is death.
To be a slave to desire is to be lost.

We have feelings in life. We need to express those feelings in a balanced way. Throughout history, there has never been anyone, including great sages who have supposedly shunned the world, who was without feeling. At the same time, there have been countless numbers who have been so carried away by their feelings that they have destroyed themselves.

Those who follow Tao teach that we cannot live in the world without feeling. Without feeling, we would not get up in the morning, move about, eat, or survive. But they also teach that we need to keep our desires simple. Too much feeling, and we become lost in the endless and ultimately destructive pursuit of pleasure.

If feelings are the color of the heart, then let us paint with the brevity and lightness of watercolor.

Laughter

Xiao. *Laughter.* Above is the word for "bamboo"; below is the word for "dog."

Just as wind shakes the leaves of the bamboo, so too do we laugh in reaction to the world.

Some ascetics do not believe in laughter. They believe laughing is a sin. Tao, however, excludes nothing, including laughter.

It is very important in understanding Tao that we perceive the transient nature of life. Everything is in a state of constant change. Therefore, we can never be complacent. We can never expect places, things, or people to remain static. If we understand that, then we have the opportunity to learn more of Tao. If we do not accept that, then madness swiftly overtakes us.

The ancients understood the ephemeral and advised their students not to take life too seriously. Life changes too quickly for us to dwell overly long on any single aspect. Things may go one way for a while, only to change quickly and unpredictably. Therefore, the wise realize that there is nothing to be gained by regarding life as immutable. It is far better to accept and work with its ephemeral quality. Then, no matter how difficult things are, we can laugh.

As nothing is permanent, there is nothing to take seriously. As there is nothing to take seriously, we should laugh at the world. As we laugh at the world, we should realize that understanding the changeable nature of life is the swiftest way to joy.

Play

Wan. *To play, toy.* On the left is jade. On the right is a phonetic and the word for "origin" or "source" (see p. 219).

Playing is as precious as jade and helps us find our way back to the beginning—the source.

What is life without play? Yes, we know we are supposed to work hard and to be disciplined if we are to live our lives well. But it takes a hard-hearted person to deny play to anyone. Maybe the hard-hearted are simply the unfortunate few who seldom have fun.

Those who follow Tao believe in fun and play. Through play, the letting go of our restrictions, the lighthearted association of disparate and "irrational" elements, the turning over of established order, we open the way to our own creativity. Many accomplishments are made by people who study carefully and put in a lot of hard work, but those who follow Tao would rather celebrate the accomplishments of those who got their best ideas while tinkering, or taking a bath, or eating breakfast, or taking a walk, or sipping tea, or just doing nothing.

A smart person takes play seriously, for in the act of playing is the possibility of going beyond established borders. And Tao, while it is everywhere, is most likely to be found outside of borders. If you want to be with Tao, it is better to put aside all that is "important" and "significant" and just play. Be natural. You'll arrive at Tao a lot sooner than if you make a "special effort."

Lining

Li. *Lining, inner, inside.* This is a compound word different in structure from the side-by-side or top-and-bottom arrangements of most words. Here, the word for "clothes," which originally was drawn to show the two sides of a robe's collar, is divided up and the phonetic is placed inside. Therefore, the word doubly implies "lining"—by the crossing-over strokes at the bottom, which are the collar, and by the placement of the phonetic inside the word for "clothes."

Those who follow Tao know that effective actions come from inner substance.

Many people would rather be the outer garment: the attractive colors, the fancy fabric, the costume presented to the world. Those who follow Tao would rather be the lining: by clinging to the inner, they not only operate on the basic level of all things, but they are protected and safe.

Without the inner structure of the lining, the outer garment would sag and lose its shape. Because the lining is on the inside, it generally outlasts the outer garment.

Thus it is with those who follow Tao. They do not crave the spotlight but work behind the scenes. They do not want to go bravely into conflict, but work instead for resolution. They do not want fame, yet they still accomplish things in life.

In their attitude toward themselves, those who follow Tao know that it is the inner that counts most. Beautiful muscles, showy clothes, and fame are quickly worn away by the tides of time. All that we have on the outside can be taken away. What we truly have on the inside can neither be taken away nor destroyed. That is why those who follow Tao always cling to the inner.

Taste

Chang. *To taste, to experience.* Below is the character for "mouth"; above is a phonetic.

Taste the world before you renounce the world.

The masters of penitence turn away from the pleasures of the world. In an attempt to subdue their desires, they even resort to self-flagellation. Tao does not agree with this. Being with Tao is about balance, not obsession.

Those who teach Tao would have us taste the pleasures of the world before giving up our desires. Neither can we give up something we don't understand, nor can we give up something before we are ready. Premature renunciation only leads to warped personalities.

The only true guideline is moderation. The charms of the world are ephemeral. They will eventually fade away, sometimes before we are ready. The mature approach is to try everything that appeals to us, maintaining reason as a counterpoint. When we have had our fill, we can let our desires go.

The toys of our childhood are a good example. Few people play with toys as adults: they had their fill of them as children and are no longer interested in them. It is instructive, however, that there are other people who collect toys or who keep some hidden away, explaining, "I was denied these while growing up." Denial breeds suppressed desire, while properly timed involvement allows us to leave behind the ties of the past and move on.

So to follow Tao requires a bit of management: we gradually taste the world so that we will be satisfied. We avoid falling into obsession. Then, when we have tasted all we want and when we no longer want anything else, we continue with Tao.

Generation

Shi. *Generation, age.* This is a compound of the number ten. A simple cross shape is combined three times to signify thirty. Thirty years represents one generation.

Tao is to be freely passed through the generations.

Tao is for everyone. No one should try to exploit Tao for his or her own ambitions. Rather, each of us who gains some appreciation for Tao should share and help others.

There was once a brilliant Taoist who became the adviser to an emperor. The Taoist's insight was so great that he controlled court intrigues and led marauding armies all over Asia. With his unsurpassed insight into Tao, he was never defeated.

They reached a walled city near Persia and gave siege to it. The residents would not surrender. The Taoist warned that unless the city gave up, he would storm it and hack off the ears of every person there. When the city remained defiant, the Taoist formulated an unbeatable strategy and brought down the defenders. Mercilessly, he ordered his threat carried out and was only satisfied when he saw a mountain of bloody ears.

Yes, Tao can be used selfishly. But what good is that? The Taoist of this story died just like anyone else. What good did he do? When you understand Tao, you too may be tempted to use it just for yourself. It's best not to try. It's far better to simply be with Tao, cherish its life-giving power, and live freely. Tao comes to each one of us freely. Pass it on freely. There is nothing to lose and everything to gain.

Dangerous

Wei. *Dangerous, peril, hazardous.* The outer left and top of this word show a person standing on a high cliff. The curled part inside the word is a phonetic.

The wise person does not reach too far. The wise person does not stand on tiptoe.

It is a challenge to avoid overextending oneself.

The essence of following Tao is to find the middle. Those who follow avoid the extremes. They seldom take absolute positions. All things have their time and their place and the wise thread a path through the middle.

It is ironic, however, that so much in life can be gained from a high vantage point. If you want to see the approach of a far-off enemy or an approaching storm, you need to go to a great overlook. But that presents the problem of exposure. Therefore, even in trying to follow a middle path, there may be times when daring is called for. Sometimes the correct decision is the one that incorporates some risk. We have to accept that. Then, we risk danger only when necessary and return to more serene circumstances as quickly as we can.

Thunder

Lei. *Thunder.* This word takes a single symbol meaning "accumulation" and triples it to signify accumulation of great magnitude. Thunder results when the pent-up energies of the clouds are suddenly released. The top part of this word adds the character for "rain."

Thunder makes us small.

Do you have any doubt as to who is supreme in this world? Certainly not human beings. Nature is greater, much greater. Even the bravest man, the richest man, the smartest man will huddle in fear when thunder and lightning are close at hand, when the fields shake and are washed away, when trees are split by bolts of searing electricity, and when the sky sounds and feels as if it is being torn to pieces.

It is good to be humble. No one has ever been able to defy thunder. No one has ever been able to exploit thunder. No one has ever been able to harness its energy. Thunder is free and powerful and overwhelming. True, people hide until it's over. No one goes out until things are peaceful again. That only underscores thunder's might.

Therefore, the ancients taught that when faced with overwhelming force, we should not confront it. When given leeway to act, we should remain circumspect.

Melt

Rong. *Melt.* On the left is the character for "water."
On the right is a phonetic.

Melting ice is seeking equilibrium. Running water is seeking its level.

When a piece of ice is put into water, it melts. It is only trying to become part of what surrounds it.

When a candle is lit, the wax melts and runs down the sides. It is only seeking its level.

When iron is heated, it melts and becomes liquid. It is only responding to the force upon it.

From observing all these things, we can gain a lesson about Tao.

Just as ice melts, we should learn to adjust to our surroundings. Nothing is possible without first establishing equilibrium.

Just as the candle melts, we must seek the lowest level in a situation. There is no need for struggle. There is no need for worry. When the flaming wick becomes too hot, the candle responds by melting and seeking a lower level.

Just as iron melts, we must be responsive to the forces that act upon us. We are not supreme in this life: the weather, time, our aging, other people, and pure chance all act upon us. Heated iron melts. It responds to the force put upon it, but it never stops being iron. When it cools, it is still metal. Thus, it both responds and remains true to itself. Those who follow Tao know the importance of combining responsiveness with integrity.

Excess

Guo. *Excess, to pass by, to cross over, to pass time, criminal.* On the left is the character for "movement" and "path." On the right is a phonetic
Excess is relative.

Following Tao is a matter of balance and moderation. Tao is the path, as the left side of the word *guo* reminds us. When we go off that path, we have the condition of excess.

Thus, those who follow Tao do not believe in absolute standards and rigid prohibitions. Everything depends on the situation. If one acts according to what the situation calls for, then one has not made any mistake. Acting with too little or too much force is a mistake. Acting without any understanding is also a mistake. Acting in betrayal of oneself is a mistake too.

Tao is like a river, and we are like boaters on the river. Those who say that to follow Tao is to surrender to it are wrong. That would be like setting one's boat adrift: sooner or later, it will hit the rocks. Those who want to imagine themselves as independent of all circumstances are like boaters who try to go upstream against a raging river: their energies will all be lost. Those who properly follow Tao are like those boaters who go with the current but still act to travel where they want.

In the first two cases, the boaters were excessive. One group did not do enough. The other did too much. The secret of Tao is not to do too little or too much. Then effortlessness will come and excess be avoided.

Sweep

Sao. *To sweep.* On the left is the sign for "hand." On the right is a phonetic, a picture of a hand holding a broom.

Sweeping is an act of humility, an act of service, and an act of meditation.

Sweep.
Do you want to know what to do with your life?
Sweep.
Do you want to know how to begin a new venture?
Sweep.
Do you want to clear away misconceptions?
Sweep.
Do you want to know how to be thorough?
Sweep.
Do you want to create order?
Sweep.
Do you want an antidote to your excesses?
Sweep.
Do you lack for something to do?
Sweep.
Do you worry about the future?
Sweep.
Do you strive to be grounded?
Sweep.
Do you find it difficult to meditate?
Sweep.
Do you find it hard to finish what you start?
Sweep.
Do you need a skill in life?
Sweep.
Do you worry too much?
Sweep.

Part Ten

DEVOTION

Offering

Li. *Offering, sacrifice, worship.* On the left is the sign meaning a revelation from heaven. On the right is the phonetic representing abundance by depicting many plants with many beans.

If you would want a revelation from heaven, you must first make an offering.

The first act of devotion is offering.

We are each on a spiritual path, and we each hope to gain the abundance of that path. But how can we gain spiritual gifts unless we are receptive? After all, nothing spiritual can occur if we are occupied with self-regard. Therefore, worship needs an act that will signify a willingness to put aside self-centered occupations in favor of receptiveness to the divine. That is why all worship involves offering.

Devotion is commitment. Through our daily acts of devotion, we demonstrate our determination to live a holy life. We cannot predict the time of our death, but we know we will die. That makes the time between the present and our death all the more important. Although that time will pass whether or not we do something valuable, it is far better to live a positive life. That is why we need offering: it signifies the commitment to lifelong devotion.

Acknowledgment becomes an act of humility and a very real understanding that what comes to us is not simply a result of our work, but a gift from Tao. Certainly, we cannot live without work, but equally, work alone will not sustain us. We live by the good fortune of what heaven and earth provide. We make our offering to show our gratitude.

Offering shows that we are receptive.
Offering shows that we are devoted.
Offering shows acknowledgment.

Flowers

Hua. *Flower.* This is a picture of a flower—the pistils and stamen are in the center, the petals are on the sides, and the base and stem are below.

Flowers are a token of life.

For all the important moments in our lives, we can barely do without flowers. When we worship at a shrine, we offer flowers. When we marry, when we die, when we are honored, when we honor others, when we console each other, we have flowers with us. When someone is ill in the hospital, we bring flowers. Isn't it because we have some sense that flowers can bring cheer and encourage life?

Flowers are beautiful. They are fragrant. They are the first burst of laughter on the plum tree at winter's end. They are the pure and unsullied beauty of the lotus, rising above the bog. They are the seductive magnificence of the peony, opening in layer after layer of exquisiteness. They are the velvety loveliness of the rose, which protects itself with sharp thorns. They are the upright character of the chrysanthemum, which blooms even as winter approaches.

A flower. The dandy twirls one in his hand, the ascetic enters into stillness while gazing at the center of one, the gardener cultivates it with love and care, the painter will lavish years in painting it, the poet will strain to describe it. Flower. So delicate. So easy to crush. So short a life.

Flowers are ephemeral. They represent life's cycles. By having them as part of our worship, we offer a part of life itself.

Incense

Xiang. *Incense, fragrance.* Above is the word for growing grain. Below is the word for "sweet." The grain is full and sweet and fragrant.
   Incense carries our prayers.

Since ancient times, in many cultures of the world incense, like flowers, has been an integral part of life. It has long been one of the precious things given as a gift. Many religions use incense in their ceremonies, and many scholars and holy people use incense as part of their contemplations.

The ancients taught that rising smoke carries our prayers to heaven. Incense is therefore both offering and vehicle. What a wonderful image: fragrant smoke carrying our delicate spiritual offerings into the empyrean sky.

Beauty and devotion are fragile in this life of violent disappointment. But for the length of time it takes for a single stick of incense to burn to its stub, we can put our hearts and minds on what is holy.

Kneel

Gui. *To kneel, to bow.* On the left is the character for "foot." On the right is a phonetic.

The higher we climb, the more circumspect we should be. The more we understand Tao, the more humble we become.

Traditionally, one knelt down before the emperor. One also knelt down before one's gods, one's teachers, one's parents, and one's spouse upon marriage. Kneeling down was a way of showing respect by demonstrating one's humility.

We don't have very many emperors left in the world, and piety—whether for gods, teachers, or parents—is also rare. However, the modesty and the respect that kneeling down signifies is not a lesson we should forget. Even boxers kneel down to give thanks after a winning bout. They know, instinctively, to be modest in victory. Those of us outside the arena should be no less humble as we give our all in the contest that is life. When we are able to reach a level of excellence, we should be grateful.

Very few people bow to one another any longer. But in the temples and monasteries and spiritual schools, the master bows to the student as if to say, "It is not I who am teaching you, but the tradition that is teaching you." And the student bows as if to say, "I know I am an ignorant disciple in need of guidance." And to each other, everyone bows to say, "I respect you." And to the gods they all bow, to say, "We always know that there are others greater than ourselves."

Learning spirituality is no harder than bending your knees.

Prayer

 Dao. *Prayer.* On the left is the sign that means "to reveal" and alludes to heaven. On the right, used phonetically, is the character for longevity (see p. 139).

Prayer is essential, but to whom do you pray?

Who are you praying to?

Prayer is a form of meditation. It is an act of reflection. When you are making an inquiry, you make it to some deep part of yourself. When you give thanks, you express gratitude for your good fortune. When you pray to another, you practice selflessness. When you pray every day, you strengthen your spirit. It takes a highly mature person to pray.

Prayer is an act of daily devotion. We who follow Tao do not pray for divine intervention, because Tao does not change its course for any human being. But that does not make prayer unnecessary. Instead, prayer becomes a way for us to see and feel Tao. And we can do that every day. And Tao is wonderful and always around us and in us. We are moved to pray, not because we want something, but because we are moved to devotion over the presence of Tao.

Sincerity

Xin. *Sincerity, faithful, belief, letter.* On the left is the character for "person." On the right is the character for "word." A person stands by his or her word and thus demonstrates sincerity.

If you want spiritual constancy, then develop sincerity.

Don't use words carelessly. Don't make promises casually. A word, once spoken, cannot be retracted. However, people love to waste words. Perhaps that is why what we say often lacks moral force.

Take this as an exercise: mean everything you say. When you give your word, always keep it. When you make a promise, fulfill it.

Keeping your word may be a difficult proposition. But only by developing this responsibility can you develop sincerity. All too often the ideas of commitment and honesty receive little consideration, and yet few of us would want to be thought of as insincere.

Sincerity is not something you can pretend to have. It comes from the integrity of standing by your word.

In the past, a vow meant something. Traditionally, no one entered into the study of Tao without making a vow. Just words. Just said once. But it determined the entire course of one's life. That is true commitment. One will never fully know Tao by casual reading and intellectual discussion. Unless you make a commitment to know it and that commitment lasts for years and years, Tao will never reveal itself fully.

If you sincerely want Tao, then vow to know it, and never waver from your commitment.

Worship

Bai. *To worship, to pay one's respect either to a deity or to another person.* This is a picture of two hands in a posture of respect and worship.

Worship requires joining left and right and acting as a whole person.

In the old scriptures, knowledge of Tao was compared metaphorically with a sacred jewel. Once this sacred jewel came into one's possession, one attained the greatest of spiritual gifts. When one is offered such a gift, one should receive it with both hands, as a sign of the greatest reverence and gratitude.

How can we accept the spiritual gift with both hands unless both hands act in cooperation?

And here is where many of us have not prepared adequately. On the left we have evil. On the right we have good. On the left we have our desires. On the right we have our aspirations. We have to come to terms with both sides of our personalities and make them work together in order to be worthy of the sacred jewel.

Notice that no one said anything about cutting off either side. Some people, perhaps, hear that one side is bad and immediately want to cut it off. That, they think, will make evil impossible. But such intentional mutilation is far from a spiritual solution. The secret of Tao is to understand all parts of oneself, even the bad, and bring them into cooperation. Then the equilibrium that is so at the heart of following Tao is made possible.

Remember, to take the sacred jewel of Tao requires both hands.

Insight

Ming. *Insight, bright, dawn, evident, open, intelligent, virtuous, enlightened.* On the left is a picture of the sun. On the right is a picture of the moon. The sun and the moon are the two brightest things; to combine them represents brightness upon brightness.

Those who unite sun and moon within themselves attain the ultimate clarity.

People imagine that spirituality is secret and hard to understand. Quite the opposite is true. Spirituality is something everyone has. The only problem is that we have been taught not to listen to the natural voice within ourselves.

People imagine that spirituality is esoteric and hoarded by masters. Quite the opposite is true. Masters would be happy if crowds flooded the temples to hear of Tao. But the temples are abandoned and the masters are dying because the world is more interested in money and pleasure.

People imagine that spirituality should be easy. Quite the opposite is true. Knowledge of Tao does not relieve the human dilemma: it clarifies it. Yet there is a world of difference between those who suffer with insight and those who suffer in ignorance. It is far better to have insight.

People imagine that spirituality requires great sophistication. Quite the opposite is true. All that is needed is to identify the polar nature of your own character and then to understand how to utilize those opposites. Once you do that, you will understand the meaning of absolute.

Therefore, to hear the natural voice within, first quiet the voices of profit and selfishness. To learn of Tao, enter into learning before all learning is gone. To live your life spiritually, gain insight into the human condition. To reach the absolute, reconcile opposites with the power of the sun and moon together.

Interval

Jian. *Interval, space, partition.* The outer part of the word is a doorway. The middle is a picture of the moon. The time when the moon shines through a doorway indicates both space and interval.

No matter where you are in life, you still have an interval of time to use wisely.

"When I die, I will rot in the ground like anyone else." There. If you say that, no priest or minister has any power over you.

So many religious leaders simply want converts. They want to build grand temples. They want obedience. They want glory. And to get that, they promise you great rewards and a guaranteed place in heaven. But we don't want that.

We want insight into this life. We want freedom to walk our way.

Therefore, we must all seek a clear, free, open path with no encumbrances. We all accept that we will die, but that means we still have to make decisions for the interval until then. We don't know how long, but that doesn't matter. The fact is, we have time, long or short. What are we going to do with that? That is the most valuable wealth we have. What will you do?

Tao is made up of many intervals strung together.

Diversity

Duo. *Diversity, many, much, overly much.* The sign for "evening" is doubled to suggest many sunsets.

Just as the moon helps us to mark time within the diversity of nights, so too should we have a central discipline before we explore others.

We can't worry every time we hear about the latest spiritual discovery. We can't worry that someone else is reaching enlightenment faster than we are.

We are increasingly aware of the many different spiritual practices all over the world. And new practices are being created out of the resulting diversity. That is right. It only stands to reason that all, even the most tradition-bound practices, were originally created at one point in time. There should be no stigma attached to spiritual practices that evolve in our lifetime—methods don't have to be from dead people in order to be valid. But once we find a way, we should stay with it resolutely and not have anxieties about other people's paths.

It is healthy to explore other disciplines. If nothing else, the elements in common can give you fresh and interesting perspectives on your own practices. But we should not flit from one discipline to another. Ecumenical explorations are fine, but they are best done from a firm base of the practices that best suit you.

Care

Quan. *To care for, to love, family.* Below is the character for "eye." Above is a phonetic, a contraction of a word that means "nourish."

To care for others is to look after them.

It is natural to care for others. If you are the one dispensing the care, then do it happily. It is really your good fortune to have someone to love and to have someone who loves you.

From animals to sages, there is care. A mother tiger, for example, will take care of her cubs. An older brother will look after the younger. Even in the temples, one monk looks after another. And the sages often looked after one another. Let us not be so concerned with our own practice that we do not look after others.

All is Tao anyway. Who is to say that the only way to be enlightened is to be sealed in a cave? Tao is movement. Tao is diverse. Our purpose is not to look for the Tao of books. Our purpose is to look for the Tao of our lives. If you have family, or children, or a spouse, or students, or classmates, or friends, then look after them. Not because you owe it to them. Not because it is the right thing to do. Not because you will get something in return. But because it is part of who you are.

Love

Ai. *To love, to delight.* Above is the sign for "person," in the center is the sign for "heart," and around it is an embracing hand.

To love is natural. To understand the variations of love is wisdom.

Love is perhaps the most powerful of human emotions. It is also the most overstated and most abused.

We need to let love be as simple as the word *ai* indicates. It is as simple as the beating of our hearts. It is expressed as easily as an embrace.

Many people want to interfere with love. Ascetics want to deny it. Perverts want to distort it. Kings want allegiance for it. Merchants want to sell it. Poets want inspiration from it. We need none of this for our hearts to beat or for our hands to reach out.

Most people would agree that love is important to them. Yet it is also one of the most vexing preoccupations in many lives. People suffer disappointments and think this is the fault of love. It isn't. Disappointments have to do with things not being perfect, with things not matching. That happens. It's hard to get things to match, even some of the time. But that has nothing to do with love. Love is all about continuing to try to get things to match. If you love, you'll continue to do that, even if that sometimes means sacrifice on your part. That's all right. Hurt and pain come as part of life. No one is exempt from it. But that is no reason not to love.

Suffering accompanies life, but love is affirmation.

Part Eleven

PERSEVERANCE

Disaster

Cai. *Disaster.* Below is the word for "fire," above is the word for "water." Fire and flood create disaster.

Disasters are not personal, but a person must be strong enough to overcome them.

One of the hardest things to accept is that disaster has nothing to do with you. You didn't do anything wrong for a natural disaster to happen. It happens on its own. Earthquakes, volcanic explosions, floods, fires, and windstorms have intention neither to harm nor to benefit.

Misfortunes happen. Nothing is learned by superstition, guilt, and fear. These only hamper a person's ability to do something. For example, climbers lost in the snows often panic, strike out on their own instead of waiting for help, and then die of exposure. The nature of their surroundings existed, whether they were there or not; the only difference between whether they were destroyed or not came solely from their response.

Misfortunes happen, and we should face them and act without fear of panic. We should learn from people who act calmly in emergencies. Heroes who rescue others in danger never speak of panic. None of them speaks of fear. None of them even speak of themselves—they don't think of their own safety and even afterward don't even regard themselves as heroes. In the view of Tao, this is ideal action. In the face of misfortune, this is complete action without the interference of fear or egotism.

Patience

 Ren. *Patience, forbearance, perseverance, suffering.* Above is a phonetic showing a knife. Below is the human heart.

One must constantly follow Tao, even though life is painful.

Life hurts. Life is painful. Life is suffering.

Yet we must go on. We must persevere. If we do, good times are sure to follow.

If we constantly seek, even in the darkness, guidance is sure to come.

If we strive against evil, no matter what the cost, then righteousness is sure to triumph.

There is nothing in life that does not involve trial. There is nothing worthwhile that doesn't have a cost. There is nothing great that does not require a series of small acts. The great triumphs over all who oppose it. To achieve that by way of small acts is supreme indeed.

It is easier to give up. It is easier to live a life of indulgence and confusion. It may be tempting simply to live like everyone else and to follow whatever society says is popular and right. But to do so is to abdicate our very lives as spiritual people. The alternative is to strive for Tao, and, yes, that striving is lonely and painful. But it is always a noble striving and an honest life. When you die, you will know what you are dying for.

So choose, because you must. Choose every day. And every day, no matter how painful and hurt and sorrowful you are, choose Tao.

Diligence

Qin. *Diligence, labor.* On the bottom is the character for "strength" (showing a muscle in its sheath). The remainder of the word is a phonetic.

One cannot go far in life without diligence.

It is useless to argue: this life is one of suffering. Nothing can be done except through our efforts.

Disasters hit all of us without meaning or explanation. Wars are constant around the globe. Family members abuse and exploit one another. Hard work is often rewarded with betrayal. The government is a haven for those who would oppress others. Despite the great wealth of information, ignorance is ever present. Money is used for selfish gains and not to help others. Spiritual leaders are often shown to be hypocrites. Homelessness is rampant. Most people do not have enough to eat. Those who have enough eat more than their share. We spend our lives looking for love, only to find bitterness. We pin our hopes to distant dreams that never materialize. We listen to teachers who tell us to work hard, only to find that the world has changed by the time we leave school. We hurt ourselves with self-doubt, low self-esteem, and slavery to desires.

Prophets disappoint us, priests befuddle us, teachers deceive us, bosses exploit us, parents reject us, spouses desert us, children are taken from us, and at the end, it is just us, staring at the grave.

This life is one of suffering. Those who don't know how to suffer are the worst off. Those who follow Tao know that there are times when things will be very difficult. That is the time to be diligent. There are times when the only correct thing we can do is to bear our troubles until a better day.

Sorrow

 Bei. *Sorrow, to grieve, sorry.* Below is the character for "heart." Above is a phonetic.
Sadness is part of being human.

People describe sorrow as a pain in the heart. They don't point to the head or anywhere else— they point to the heart. Everyone feels sadness.

The ancients believed that different parts of the body held different emotions. But just as we need all our organs in order to be whole and functioning, so too must we accept all emotions as part of the cohesive and balanced whole of our inner lives. Every emotion has a function, and all of them together contribute to our actions.

Our emotions are not learned; they are inherent. An infant, in the first hours after birth, already has emotions. Throughout childhood, it is apparent that children's feelings remain integral parts of their personalities. We cannot destroy our emotions any more than we can live without organs. So the best thing to do is to accept them and the role they play in our lives.

When sadness comes, we have to accept it. It is here. It is part of our life. We cannot negate it. We cannot avoid it. We need not think that there is something wrong with us if we feel sad. We should accept it as something indelible and necessary.

No one likes sadness. But it plays a part in our lives, just as any one of our organs plays a part. But while sadness is indelible, it is not predominant either. Other emotions exist too, and they will inevitably follow sadness. Therefore, those who follow Tao seek to find any advantage sadness may offer.

Inch

 Cun. *Inch*. The dot represents the pulse, located on the arm about an inch from the hand.

We are our own measure.

When life is filled with adversity and everything seems to be against you, remember your goals.

You may be poor, you may be alone, you may be ill, you may be oppressed. But no matter what your circumstances, you always have volition. Take advantage of that.

Why be so proud that you refuse to take little steps when little steps are all that you can do? If you cannot make grand strides, at least try to move an inch. An inch in one direction, then an inch in another already make up a span of two inches. Gradually, we can improve upon that. We need patience, and we need to know where we are going, but if we remember the significance of an inch, then we always have room to move.

Look at a redwood. It does not grow to its height all at once. It goes little by little. So slowly and so gradually do its roots move that it can find a toehold even in seemingly solid rock. In time, with its inch-by-inch movements, that redwood can split granite and still find sustenance for itself. At the same time, the redwood moves inch by inch upward and expands inch by inch in girth. Given enough time, the tree can outlive many creatures on earth by generations and attain a stature difficult to uproot.

The redwood does not disdain the tactics of the inch. How can we?

Endure

Shou. *To endure, to receive, to suffer, to bear, to inherit, to succeed to.* Below is the sign for the right hand. Above is another hand, handing something to the lower hand.

To endure is not just to suffer without meaning; often there is a gift in suffering.

You will be stripped of everything at least once in your life. The ability to bear that torture makes all the difference between survival and capitulation.

We can endure if we know how life works and if we know ourselves thoroughly. If we accept suffering without reliance on unrealistic notions of divine judgment or the idea of retribution for past lives, we will be able to last through the difficulties with our eyes fully open. We might even learn something. But that comes only when we face the travails of life without flinching.

Grappling with fate is like meeting an expert wrestler: to escape, you have to accept the fall when you are thrown. The only thing that counts is whether you get back up. Keep getting back up. With enough experience, you can become a good wrestler. You will suffer much, but there will be a reward. Life is that way too. Endure, and you will get better.

Endurance yields a gift: you learn who you are by the toughest of trials.

Doubt

 Huo. *To doubt, to mislead.* Below is the character for "heart" or "mind." Above is a phonetic. It shows a small square representing a mouth combined with the symbol for "weapon." Words combined with "weapon" suggest a threat.

When one has doubts, it is usually because there have been attempts to mislead.

When a religious leader urges you to be spiritual for the sake of a place in heaven, ask yourself: Are you a child who needs to be bribed to do the right thing?

When a teacher says that you should enter Tao so that you can become immortal, ask yourself: Why search far afield when the glory of Tao is always at hand?

When a master exhorts you to be pure and avoid divine punishment, ask yourself: Who needs threats in order to know purity?

When an authority tells you that to be religious is to be better than everyone else, ask yourself: Who needs the illusion of superiority?

Spiritual leaders are supposed to be leading us to truth and instead they use exaggerations to gain converts.

Or do they believe these things themselves?

Ruin

Huai. *To ruin, to spoil.* On the left is the character for "earth." On the right is a phonetic meaning "to hide," symbolized by a child covered with clothing (see p. 145 for a similar compound for the word "clothing" with another word inside it). When something was buried, it was ruined.

Before one undertakes to mound things up, one would be well advised to consider how easily ruin comes.

It is said that the palace of the First Emperor of China was larger than any palace ever built before or since. It took a messenger three days to go by horse from front to back. A hundred thousand soldiers guarded it. Each of its pillars was fashioned from a single tree trunk ten spans in diameter, and its rooftops were sheathed in bronze.

But the kingdom was ruined due to the First Emperor's imprudence. Enemies attacked and ransacked the palace. They burned it down. It took three months to burn it completely.

Before we undertake monumental tasks, it would be wise to consider ruin. Eventually, all things will fall to the earth, as the word *huai* reminds us. A grand palace invites attack by enemies. Great emperors may have great tombs but they end up under the ground like anyone else.

Therefore, look at the word *huai*. Take away that cloth shielding your eye to see the true Tao.

Gain

Li. *Gain, profit, prosperity.* The left side of the word shows grain. The right side shows a knife. When the grain is harvested, wealth comes.

Some people might say it is hard to pursue Tao without the gain to support one's endeavors. But it's important to distinguish the exact types of gain that will actually bring us profit.

In the beginning, the ancients taught very simple and direct ways to live with Tao. But as time went on, people embellished the teachings until they became a very complicated body of knowledge that took a thousand volumes to document. Tao became the pursuit of the rich and cultured. Only they could afford the herbs, the lessons, the expensive art materials, the beautiful living locations, the servants, the travel, and the myriad other luxuries that afforded the freedom to pursue Tao. For many centuries, the simple and rustic ideals of the ancients were obscured by wealth, alchemy, artistic pursuits, and eccentricity.

We who want Tao may imagine that we will never succeed if the wealth and cultured living of the past are required. But that is not so. Do not be misled by the trappings of those who lived in the past. Look instead to what actually exists in your own life. As long as you live and breathe, as long as your heart beats and your mind dwells on the way, Tao can be found.

If we look at the image of gain, there is a lesson for us. Gain is simply the result of harvest. We don't need a fancy lifestyle. We need know only where to look for grain and when to harvest it. Those who harvest the ordinary are those who ultimately gain.

Single

Tan. *Single, odd, thin.* This is a word that is opposite in meaning to its picture. Above is a phonetic. Below is a symbol for three armies (possibly derived from a depiction of war chariots), meaning "war."

One should not hesitate to embrace the solitary in order to find Tao.

The ascetics of Tao, although they were not personally wealthy, were surrounded by friends and country folk who knew and respected their goals and who supported them. All these holy people owned was one patched robe and a begging bowl, but they were still part of a community. They could wander anywhere they pleased and they could find lodging at any temple they stopped at for the night, because these temples were supported by patrons, worshipers, and the emperor. In such cases, people could trust themselves to Tao since they could be assured of food, shelter, companionship, learning, and reverence wherever they went.

Today, we live in a disjointed world. The communities that supported Tao no longer exist. Frequently, when one wants to live a life of Tao, one finds oneself alone and without support. It's hard to find teachers, hard to find temples, hard even to find a quiet spot to meditate.

But being a follower of Tao is to be accepting. If we are poor, if we find ourselves frustrated by the disparity between our ideals and our circumstances, if we find it difficult to find the guidance we need, let us acknowledge it, let us accept it, but let us not be deterred. For the true Tao cannot be bought.

Who is to say? We are who we are, and who we are is always good enough. Even if we have to be solitary our whole lives, we must pursue Tao.

Fate

Ming. *Fate, destiny, life.* The top three lines form a triangle to give the idea of union or an assembly. The lower right corner shows a seal being applied to the joined lines: a decree. The square on the lower left is a mouth giving an order. Destiny is life's irresistible decree.

That which is decreed in our lives must be obeyed, but, like heaven, it changes constantly.

Nothing is literally preordained. There is no cosmic force manipulating us at every moment of the day. We cannot predict how the water at the head of the river will make a current at the mouth, but we can know the general course of the river's flow. We know the banks of the river, but what will happen along each mile of that river is still unknown.

So too it is with life. We are journeying on its river, and we don't know what will be around each bend for us. Others have charted it, others have made poetry, history, commerce, and war on its waters and shores, but what will each of us do? That is not yet known.

However, the idea that fate is neither static nor absolute does not absolve us from the need to understand life. Fate is a metaphor both for our actions and our surroundings. What we do does count for the future: our actions today determine our later choices. And our surroundings affect us too: they give us a certain range of opportunities from which to select.

Perhaps the hardest lesson to learn in life is to accept our limitations. But instead of thinking of them as a preordained set of conditions, we have to understand them on a much more subtle level. Our "fate" is a constantly fluid set of limitations created by the interaction of our decisions and our opportunities. We can neither transcend them nor can we regard them as boundaries that will never change. Fate is constantly changing and yet we can never ignore it. Coming to terms with that is the secret of happiness.

Recovery

 Quan. *To be cured, recovery from illness.* The bracket-shaped part of the word on the top and left is the sign for "illness"—it is a combination of roof above, with the sign for "bed" on the left (when one is ill, one stays at home and takes to bed). Below the horizontal line, on the lower right, is a phonetic character that is the sign for "completeness."

When illness is overcome, recovery is complete.

Can we see illness as an opportunity?

Is it the medicine and the treatment that cure us, or do we cure ourselves? It's like the old joke about the cure for a cold. If you take medicine, you'll recover in a week, but if you simply rest, you'll get better in seven days.

Whenever we're sick, our bodies have to find the means to destroy the illness and recover health. There is a learning process and a creative process. No one has ever invented a medicine that duplicates the body's talents. A vaccine alone doesn't make you immune to a disease. It gives your body the impetus to create its own antibodies.

Therefore, minor illnesses are not occasions of malaise, but the necessary time to create our own cure. It is a not a moribund sign, but a wonderful sign of health.

Remembering

Qi. *To remember, to record.* The left side is the sign for "words" or "to speak." The right side is a phonetic, the sign for "self."

To remember Tao each day is to act upon Tao each day.

It's hard to get up each day and keep one's mind on Tao. A hundred responsibilities weigh on us. We have to work. We have to keep our appointments. There are bills to be paid. Family members need help. Something in our house needs to be repaired.

At the same time, the daily news brings stories more bizarre and stressful than anything a fiction writer—no, let's make that a horror writer—could concoct. Going out on the street brings the uncertainty of kidnapping, assault, and accident. Just to keep up with the developments of society, we have to digest an incredible amount of information: news about the government, stocks, the environment, the weather, prices in the marketplace, and war—from a combination of radio, television, print media, and electronic networks. Then we have to make contact with the world too. People demand our responses by letter, by phone, by fax, by modem, and in person.

And in the middle of all this, we're supposed to remember to be spiritual?

Yes.

It is a challenge to search for Tao, even in the plethora of phenomena that happen to us each day. We can see the phenomena of the world as distractions or we can see them as rich in meaning. Like the word *qi,* meaning is to be found in the relation between the information passed to us and the self.

Distance

Yuan. *Distant, far.* On the left is the sign for "path" or "movement." The remainder of the word is a phonetic and means "long robe." Some say that this means that a person who is traveling is seen from a distance and so only the robe is visible. Other suggest that this represents a long robe for a distant journey.

To travel far on a path: that is the definition of distance. To travel far in one's body—our robe—is to live long.

When older people look at younger ones, they often think back over their own youth, and how far away it is. Would they change places? Would they go back if they could? Some would. Others would adamantly refuse.

Many people say: "If I could go back to being young—only knowing everything I know now—it would be great!" But would it? To go back in time, to have the vitality and also the limitations of youth with the added pressure of knowing exactly what was happening to you—maybe that's not worth it.

When older people look at young ones, they see how far the young have to go. Yes, they have years of excitement and new possibilities before them. Yes, they do not have the pains and scars that the elders do. Yes, life is adventuresome and joyous. But they don't know how far they have to go.

The old look at the tender children and lament the hurt that will be unavoidable. They look at them, and then they know distance.

There are people older and people younger than each of us. We are all somewhere in the middle of our journey. Let us freely admit that what is to come is still a mystery. Probably that's the way it is meant to be. We all have greater wisdom than we did in our younger years. And we all have a blindness to the predicaments still to come in our journey. Maybe that "ignorance" is all that keeps us sane.

Inner

Nei. *Inner, within, inside.* The angle shape at the top means "to enter." The upside down U shape of the remainder of the word represents a room or a house.

The ability to persevere comes only from inner strength.

The ability to persevere comes from inside ourselves. Nothing outside can give it to us. When circumstances are against us, when life tries us to our very core, when all other resources are closed to us, we must have an inner well from which we can draw power. It is like a castle in ancient times besieged by attackers. If it has its own well and its own provisions, it can hold fast until aid comes. The difference between survival and destruction is often the difference between how strong one's inner resources are.

People look at the methods of following Tao and wonder why there is so much emphasis on preparing and training oneself. After all, the standards of the ancients are so much higher than what is normally regarded as necessary. This need for inner strength is one of the most compelling reasons for study. Life is not given to us, and fortune comes and goes without any warning. Therefore, it is wisdom to have the inner reserves to withstand the lassitudes of life. It is only our inner will and energy that can be stronger than misfortune.

The wisdom of Tao is to know the flow of the outer world. But the genius of Tao is to establish and sustain the inner force of a person. That is our only hope of lasting long enough to follow Tao to the end.

Hope

Wang. *To hope, to expect, to look toward, the full moon.* The upper left quadrant is a phonetic. The upper right quadrant represents an eye. The lower part of the word shows a person standing on the earth. A person who searches far hopes for a particular result.

Nothing can be done without hope.

We all need hope. Without it, we would not go on to tomorrow. All the fancy words of philosophy, all the rationalizations of theology will not change our need to keep going. Talking about theories fulfills intellectual needs. But to get up each day, to work for what we believe in, to put our will toward accomplishments important to us—none of that is possible without hope.

Hope requires a goal. If we did not have a goal to aim for, like the person searching in the word *wang*, we could not have hope. Hope is that belief that helps us imagine our goals and inspires us to work toward them.

Hope is also our reaction to pain. We suffer, but in our suffering we sense that there is some way out of our pain, and we search for that opening. Thus, we are moved to find Tao, for with it comes the possibility of a better life.

Have something to hope for.

Make yourself into a person who can attain that hope.

And when you have hope, share it with those you meet. We need more hope in the world.

Part Twelve

TEACHING

Ask

Wen. *To ask, to inquire.* The square in the center represents a mouth. Around it is a door. To ask is to go to someone's door to make an inquiry.

You ask in order to enter the spiritual gate.

Those who want to study spirituality go to a
master.
Those who go to a master must inquire.
When one wishes to hear the temple bell, one must lift the
stick.
When one goes to an oracle, one must ask a question.
Those would want to enter a spiritual path must first ask.

Too many people think that because they have been lucky in life, the spiritual answers should present themselves as easily. But life is not that way. Nothing that is worth having is easy to get. That counts most of all for the spiritual.

To gain the spiritual path requires effort and self-discipline. The secret is that the greatest spiritual obstacle lies within us. It is like going to war but finding that the enemy is a traitor within our own ranks. Naturally, this type of enemy is the most difficult to fight, because it knows our every move and can strike us without being hindered by distance. In the same way, we undercut our own spiritual aspirations, an inclination we need help to overcome.

But trying to overcome our own faults leaves us with a dilemma. It is like a compassionate general who wants to find an assassin hidden in a city without harming the populace. In the same way, we have to subdue the demon within us without harming ourselves. That is difficult indeed, and for that we need help. And to get help, we must always be willing to ask.

Master

Shi. *Master, leader, teacher.* The left half of the word is a phonetic representing a place or territory. The character on the right is a picture of a banner. The leader must have a banner to direct followers.

The master is the embodiment of Tao.

There was once a student who wanted to enter Tao. Upon hearing of a famous master, he went into the mountains and searched far and wide. But the sage was elusive, and the student continued to search for years.

After a time, the student chanced upon a hut deep in the forest. Inside was a small altar, a few scrolls, and several books so esoteric that the student was unable to decipher them. The kitchen was small—a hearth and a jar of water—and the only furnishings were a rough wooden table and a small bed. The student waited for days by that hut, but no one came.

Year after year, the student returned to the hut. Each time it was empty. But he was encouraged because sometimes the stove was warm, and other times the scrolls had been changed.

After decades, the student had forgotten all about his search and was content merely to wander the trails. Lost in thought, he arrived at the hut. As usual, it was empty and, thinking this day no different from any other, he went in. After only a few moments, the old master walked in.

Instantly, the man fell to his knees and asked the master to accept him. The teacher nodded, saying only that conditions must have been right for them to meet and he was, therefore, accepting the student without further discussion. The master knew, of course, that it was the years of searching, not the techniques he would pass on, that formed the true basis of learning.

There are still a few masters today, but they are hard to find. They may be recalcitrant, they may be irritable, they may be difficult. They may say nothing for the first few times you meet them. You should not be fooled, however. Inside, the master is noting your reactions and sensing what is needed from the encounter. If you make the mistake of judging everything at face value, you miss a great opportunity.

Crazy

Feng. *Crazy, leprosy, paralysis.* The bracket-shaped part on the top and left is the sign for sickness (see p. 179). The word on the inside is the character for "wind." This word plays a phonetic role here, but may also allude to traditional beliefs that illnesses, including madness, were caused by evil "winds" that entered a person.

Those who follow Tao appear to be crazy because the spirit of Tao is in them.

In olden times, those who followed Tao were called crazy. Some were filthy beggars who went around muttering to themselves. Others lived in silent mountain abodes, never talking to anyone. Still others were drunk artists, shouting and muttering while wildly flinging ink.

Without a doubt, most of those who followed Tao in the past were highly educated and cultivated people. It's just that the ancient masters saw through the futility of social accomplishments and operated on a mental level so deep that they appeared quite mad. But most weren't. They were simply interested in levels of human existence so far beyond the common perception that they appeared crazy. In cases where the teachers were bothered by shallow petitioners seeking secrets of immortality or details of political strategy, they might even have feigned madness in order to be left alone.

But which is worse, the madness of following Tao or the madness of an existence without awareness?

Good

Hao. *Good, right, very.* On the left is a picture of a woman. On the right is a picture of a child in swaddling clothes. "Good" is synonymous with the care that a mother shows for a child.

Whoever you learn from, make sure he or she is a good person.

While it is true that the masters of Tao are eccentric and test their students, difficult personalities are not by themselves a sign of mastery. It is very important to note that, above all, a master must be a good person. That means a master cares for the student, as a mother does for a child. The master must be gentle, as a mother is with a child. The master puts the needs of the student before all else, as a mother does for a child.

Throughout history, there have been many teachers who abused their students. There were others who ruined the minds of their students, so that the young would not surpass them. There were others who simply used their positions in order to bolster themselves and secure a livelihood. These are not the kinds of people from whom you should learn. Unfortunately, they outnumber true masters by a hundred to one. It is therefore important that you search as long as necessary and as carefully as possible. You should treat your own spiritual life with the same care that a mother shows her child. After all, you are seeking someone to train the most intimate and innocent part of yourself.

Use the same care in choosing a master for yourself as you would in choosing a teacher for your child. In both cases the stakes are the same: a good master can bring forth hidden talents. A bad master can plant evil seeds that can never be uprooted, even in a lifetime.

Spiritual

Ling. *Spiritual, spirit, divine, intelligent.* The top half of the word is a picture of rain falling from a cloud. In the middle are three squares, representing a crowd of people. At the bottom is a representation of two shamans who are dancing to bring the rain.

One practices, to bring Tao into oneself as rain falls onto the earth.

There is a famous *guzheng* (zither) teacher who in her everyday life drives a van, cooks her own dinner, and goes to movies. On her way to the stage, she consults with the producers, counsels her nervous students, and jokes with her friends. Her demeanor changes as she sits with her instrument, however, her hands hovering over the strings. A calm comes into her, and she gives herself over to the music.

There is a famous opera singer who loves to eat, giggles freely, and takes the bus to her performances. She says part of her fears she will not remember all the words when she sings. She admits that this part of her watches the other part of her sing the arias flawlessly. Her admirers describe her singing as being like spontaneous improvisation.

There is a priest who was asked to demonstrate painting and calligraphy in the middle of a social gathering. He had just been talking of worldly events. Although tired, he agreed. He prepared ink, brush, and paper, and then paused. His gregariousness disappeared and a look of inner euphoria came over him. His calligraphy showed a rare vitality only possible with unerring movement.

There is a boxer who jokes with his comrades, telling everyone he can barely remember his name, let alone his footwork. But when he enters the ring, his face changes, and his body moves in a suddenly feline way, as if something had entered into him and was moving his body.

They say that Tao is spiritual. They say that the divine spirit, the *ling,* can enter into you. Why should this be believed? Because mastery is there for those who can see it.

Come

Lai. *To come, in the future.* This is a combination of the number ten (the large cross shape) with three signs for the word "person"—many people are coming.

The right guidance comes at the right time.

There is a saying common to many spiritual traditions: "When the student is ready, the teacher will come." The search is just as critical as the meeting.

The search prepares us mentally and tests us. Are we sincere? Do we really want to study? Or is it simply an infatuation? In virtually any spiritual tradition, we can find stories of disciples who weren't ready, or weren't capable, or weren't sincere. Simply entering into a spiritual path is no guarantee of success. From that perspective, the arduousness of the search is part of how we come to understand our motivation and how the master will come to know our sincerity.

The search is also how we narrow down what we really want to study. Education is, in part, experiment. We want to uncover the knowledge and techniques that will best resonate with our souls. If the bell of our soul is never struck, how will we know the pitch and duration of its sound? So we have to search. Our experiences strike us, like the stick hitting the bell, and we learn about ourselves.

The search for a teacher is more difficult than finding a mate—and we all know how tough finding a mate can be. It is not simply a matter of saying, "You're a famous teacher, well known for your powers and your ability to awaken Tao in your students, so take me." No, you have to feel comfortable with each other, you have to *like* each other, feel a kinship with one another. Then the possibilities of success are much greater.

"When the student is ready, the teacher will come." This phrase is true. The search is how you become ready. Rest assured, that for the "ready" person, Tao can be known in a moment. With just a word or a gesture, a teacher can awaken all of Tao in a student—if that student is truly ready.

Ounce

Liang. *Ounce, pair.* This is a picture of a Chinese ingot of gold or silver. Two of these ingots made a Chinese ounce.

An ounce of strength is all it takes to influence balance.

The masters understand balance well. How could they not? So much of understanding Tao comes down to a matter of balance.

Look at a child learning to walk. In the beginning, balance is difficult and falls are inevitable. Even when some steps are taken, they are wild, rocking, and unstable. Not so with an experienced adult. She has mastered balance and can maintain it even when surprised.

Thus, the masters grow very sensitive to minute shifts, and they know how to equalize any situation. They do not rely on strict rules or even the prevailing conceptions of society. They look at a situation and see what is required, and then add that regardless of what conventional thinking might recommend.

One ounce of strength is often all that is needed to bring the scales into balance. Scales don't always need to be balanced by piling on big rocks. Where matters of the spirit are concerned, subtlety counts for much. Therefore, a student should never despair if the right master has not yet been found or if learning seems to be going slowly. The master will know exactly when and where to place the right amount of weight. The master will look at the student and suggest ways in which the student can improve most rapidly. The suggestions may be oddly simple, but sometimes, that is all that is needed.

Difficult

Nan. *Difficult, distress.* On the left is the sign for a short-tailed bird. On the right is a phonetic that is itself a sign for a bird too. The original meaning of this word is unknown, and no one knows how this compound came to be borrowed to mean "difficult."

When the sustaining power of spiritual teaching is offered to us, we should accept it and use it even if the way is difficult.

There was once a master who had many talented students, each of whom he offered to teach a special knowledge. The youngsters began eagerly, but one by one, they left the master without completing their studies. One complained that he could not stand the isolation. Another disliked all the reading. Yet another wanted to get married instead. And another was called back home to care for an ailing parent.

So we may bemoan our fate that we cannot find a teacher, but there is no guarantee that we will be ready to make the commitment to study. Mastery of Tao is difficult, and the way is arduous. That is why the classics constantly emphasize the importance of perseverance. You think it is easy to study Tao, but really it is the most difficult thing you will ever try to do. You can always leave a job. College is over in four years. If you don't like where you live, you can move. But to study Tao—that is an open-ended and lifelong commitment. You have to follow the constantly changing Tao forever.

Knowledge of Tao will not necessarily make your life easier. You have to go to sleep at night, you have to wake up the next morning, and you have to keep right on being a human being. You will not become supernatural, and if no one was doing it before, no one will bring you breakfast in bed. Don't think that Tao will make your life easier. It might even do the opposite.

The only difference is that you will have more awareness.

Instruct

 Xun. *To instruct, to teach, to persuade.* On the left is the sign for "word." On the right is the sign for "river." Words of instruction are as abundant and flowing as a river.

The correct teaching is like flowing water. Flowing water should nurture, not destroy.

In the word *xun,* instruction is compared to a flowing river.

Many teachers think only of themselves. They want to be admired. They are like a dangerous and raging river.

Other teachers are pious, but so love their own learning that they cannot bear to make it accessible, even to their students. Great knowledge, they say, can never be compromised. They are like a river too wide to cross.

The best teachers think only of the student. They bring out the best in the student, regardless of their own inclination, and work to convey knowledge in a way the student can absorb. They are like a life-giving stream.

Those who are teachers in Tao therefore uphold this ideal. It doesn't matter if the teacher is famous for a certain subject; if the student doesn't need that, the teacher will teach what the student needs. It doesn't matter if knowledge is infinite; the teacher will begin the student on the path to exploration so that he or she is never left confused and lost. It doesn't matter if the time grows long; the teacher is patient and nurtures the student through all the stages of the student's learning.

The teacher who brings out the best in the student is the greatest master.

Ache

Teng. *Ache, pain.* The symbol on the top and left stands for "illness." On the lower right is a phonetic that is the word for "winter."

    We ache, because that is human. To learn from it, that is wisdom.

You, great teacher:
Did you ever suffer loneliness?
Did you ever have doubts?
You sit on the dais
Like a god fully formed.
Have we anything in common—
You in your glory,
We in our misery?

Where in the classics
Is there simple empathy for the human struggle?
Where in the deep philosophies
Do they speak of the fragile heart?
Neither chants nor rituals help,
The road ahead cannot be seen.
There is nothing to do but walk on
And contemplate again at the next vista.

Nurture

Yang. *To nurture, to rear.* Below is the character "to eat." Above is a phonetic and the character for "lamb."

To nourish is to feed with the docility of a lamb.

If you are a parent or a teacher, nurture your children well. They are young, innocent, too small even to harbor big dreams or evil intent. You know how bad the world is. You know there are no absolutes. You know how frightening life can be. But if you are ever to make your children independent, you have to love them and nurture them without reserve.

The lamb is a symbol of devotion and docility. Gentleness should be every parent's and teacher's standard. Sure, life is tough. Sure, you never had it as good as today's young. But isn't it time someone had it good and right? Maybe it's too late for us. But it isn't too late to create some good feelings and hope in someone else.

Good parents not only nurture children with food, they nurture them emotionally, intellectually, and spiritually as well. The most important thing they can do is simply to be *present*. It is not a matter of quality time. It is a matter simply of time. The best thing you can do is just to be there as often and as long as possible. If you can always be present for your child, then your child will understand what presence and constancy are. There is no way to teach this other than by example.

Some masters in old schools withheld their "secrets" in fear that their students would surpass them. With such selfishness, it is no wonder that their lineages have died out. What do you, as the elder, have to fear by teaching all you know? The child can never "catch up" to you. But if you teach without holding back, then the child may someday extend what you have passed on.

It is in the selflessness of nurturing that the nurturer is in turn nurtured.

Father

Fu. *Father.* This is a picture of a hand holding a scythe. The children see their father returning from the fields.

If you despair of the distance between yourself and those who are older than you in Tao, you need only realize that they had to walk the same path.

It may be very difficult for you to understand, but your teachers, parents, and masters had to go through exactly the same stages in life that you must go through. They all came from a woman's womb. They all had to wear diapers, and cry for milk, and learn to crawl. They all had the pain of growing teeth, they all had to learn how to relieve themselves on their own, be weaned, and learn to sleep alone. They all had to learn how to be with others. They all had to go to school and struggle with their lessons. They all had to cope with the bullying of others and the need to protect those who were weaker. They all had to face the anxieties of the future, the need for a livelihood, the need to face the death of those around them, and the need to plot a course for themselves. Literally without any exception, every single person older than you had to go through the same things you are going through.

So if you want to know what being older is like, look at your father. If you want to know your origins are and gain an impression of what your psychological and spiritual legacies are, look at your father. If you want to know what the future is like, look at your father.

And if you would want to know whether you can succeed in knowing Tao, just look at your spiritual parent, who is your master. The fact that he or she started with nothing and attained spiritual insight is your guarantee that it is also possible for you.

The wise look at the patterns but do not feel confined by them.

Verify

 Shi. *To verify, to test.* On the left is the symbol for "words." On the right is a phonetic, the word for "pattern."

Verify what you learn.

Life is very short. We all want to live it well. We study spiritual systems in search of techniques and traditions to help us live our lives better.

While there is no shortage of people purporting to be sages, there is certainly ongoing confusion about which system to follow. Why? After you subtract all the false masters interested only in their own veneration and support; after you subtract all the religions paralyzed by dogma, ritual, and politics; after you subtract the systems where secrets are not readily shared; after you subtract the traditions ruined by supposed reform; and after you subtract the teachings subverted by people who never learned how to put theory into action—after you subtract all these things, there is very little left. To find the kernels of truth is hard indeed.

That is why you must look beyond mere fame. Do the teachings work or not? If the masters say practice this and the gods will appear before you in a hundred days, see if it happens. If they tell you to practice ten years to attain enlightenment, then wait the ten years. The point is, however, that the teachings must work for you in your life and your time. It is absolutely worthless to accept a teaching on mere faith, or because a book says to, or because everyone is doing it. None of that matters. All that matters is that the teachings work for you. And if they do, then faith is never a difficult matter.

Part Thirteen

SELF

Oneself

 Zi. *Oneself*. This is a picture of a nose. Originally the picture was of the entire face, but it was eventually simplified to just a nose.

All spirituality begins and ends with the self.

In the ancient times, there was a man who decided that he might commit himself to being a spiritual person, if only he could see the gods. After all, he reasoned, most people worshiped mere images. He needed to see the actual gods before he would believe.

He began by visiting temples. At each location, the masters told him that if he wanted to see the gods, he had to go on to another temple farther away. The man did so. After visiting a hundred temples, the masters told him that the gods he sought could perhaps be seen at holy sites where spectacular historical events had occurred, and so he undertook many years of pilgrimage. He was already middle-aged, but he still wanted to see the gods.

Someone told him that the mountain sages were the only ones who saw gods, and so he shifted his search to the high peaks and visited hermit after hermit. He wandered all across a continent, through mountain ranges and across wide deserts. Finally, when he was old and white-haired, he trekked long into the Himalayas and finally found a solitary ascetic. He presented his goal to the sage, who responded with a chuckle. "If you want to see the gods," he said, "just sit down and close your eyes." The man did so and was instantly enlightened.

All answers are already within the self.

Person

Ren. *Person.* The picture shows a human figure in profile. Often the words for "heaven," "earth," and "person" form a phrase summing up the totality of the universe.

A person is part of nature and nature is part of a person.

Tao is everything. There is nothing that is not Tao.

A person is part of Tao. And a person is completely made up of Tao.

Therefore, we can follow Tao anywhere we go, but we can also follow Tao through introspection. We are Tao. And if we want to know more about Tao, we need to learn more about ourselves.

The ancients drew pictures of human beings, just the same as they drew pictures of anything else. We were seen as part of all nature. And all of nature was seen as a part of us. It was natural for us to seek Tao, for it was natural that we wanted to learn.

The only true error that human beings make is this: we imagine ourselves to be separate from Tao. It is due to this single mistake and this single mistake alone that we are ignorant.

When we divorce ourselves from Tao, we put ourselves in conflict with it. That is a losing proposition, but we imagine we can get away with it. Only Tao will catch up to us eventually, and we will find ourselves not only in an unfortunate position, but with no insight either.

Heart

Xin. *Heart, mind.* This is a simple picture of a human heart.

The heart is the center of our body from which truth emanates.

The ancients never made any distinction between the heart and the mind. In the ancient script, the two are synonymous. This point cannot be overemphasized, and you will understand the ancient scriptures a hundred times better if you remember that the heart and mind were regarded as one.

The ancients did not separate mind and body, so they did not separate thinking from emotion.

They did not separate idea from action.

They did not separate logic from intuition.

By seeing the mind as synonymous with the heart, they avoided a thousand philosophical problems. We who forget that the heart and mind are one can solve a thousand daily problems by remembering the single word: heart.

Body

Shen. *Body, torso, oneself, pregnant, personal, one's whole life.* The word shows a human figure in profile with a large abdomen and one foot forward for firm equilibrium.

The body is the firm foundation for the mind.

Those who follow Tao make no duality of the body and mind. If they say, "Look within," the natural starting point is the body. You start there and eventually you can reach the mind, then the soul, then Tao. For the sake of discussion, we talk about these different parts of a human being, but in the view of Tao, they are parts of an indivisible whole.

Different schools have different methods, but all of them agree that the body and mind are part of a continuous whole. One school believes in focusing only on a point inside the body below the navel. Another posits seven centers, from the base of the torso to the crown. Others follow the flow of the meridians. Some merely watch their inhalations and exhalations. Whatever the school, they believe that the body is the gateway to the profound.

Some people have said, "I'd like to study Tao, but I don't want to start out with all the physical exercise. Maybe I'll just learn a little meditation and philosophy." But that isn't the way to do it. Following Tao is not just a matter of intellectuality. Following Tao requires a transformation of the body, mind, and spirit. Then one has a chance to sense Tao.

You

Ni. *You.* This is an early form of the word, derived from a contraction of the words meaning "beauty." The modern form of this word is completely different.

The names that others say are you are not necessarily who you are.

When you were born, you were naked. Your parents gave you a name, because you did not come with one.

Then process of socialization began: name at birth, records, address, school, accomplishments, career. It was a necessary evil, one that we perpetuate. We can see it in the rightly dreaded ritual of small talk: "What's your name? What do you do for a living? Are you married? Children? How old are you? Where are you from?"

Following Tao is the opposite of all these questions.

Those who follow Tao undo all of this. They want to uncover again the original nature they had when they were born. Then they want to go back and see the nature they had before they were born.

In public, we may be pursuing our responsibilities. In our private time, we put all that aside and try to return to the source. In that returning, we no longer have names, we no longer have anything credited to us. We are who we are, and no more. But who we are at that point: that is truth.

Me

Wo. *I, me.* This is a person holding a spear. Possibly the word was borrowed. Its original meaning is now lost.

The very idea of the self implies conflict and defense. Who holds the spear, and what is the original nature of that person?

As soon as someone comes to close to us, we loudly shout for them to get away. If they don't, we pick up our spear to drive them off.

After the conflict, what do we do? We tensely mull over our fright and indignation and prepare for greater conflicts. When they come back, we say, "I'll show them."

The sages would ask us what we have to be so defensive about. If we were truly to inquire into the nature of things, we would see that there is nothing that we can truly lose, so there is nothing that we need to defend. What they mean is that the self is only something that we cling to as a convenient and pragmatic way of thinking, but it is not reality.

What is the reality of the self?

Inquire on one level, and you will see we are all gods.

Inquire more deeply, and you will see we are all spirit.

Inquire more deeply still, and you will see we are all Tao.

Inquire deepest of all, and you will see that Tao is the void.

And what need is there to pick up a spear and try to defend the void?

Others

Ta. *He, she, them, others, it.* On the left is the character for "person." On the right is a phonetic.

We should not define ourselves by how others define us.

You call me by a name. You write to me at a certain address. When you check with the government, you find a history. You say I was born in a certain nation and therefore I must have a certain cultural understanding. You say that I have done business, that I am a citizen, that I am of a certain race, that I am of a certain gender, that I have a family. Therefore, you think these features are me.

You call yourself by a name. You give out a certain address. When someone checks with the government, they find a history. You say you were born in a certain nation and therefore you have a certain cultural understanding. You say that you have done business, that you are a citizen, that you are of a certain race, that you are of a certain gender, that you have a family. Therefore, you think these features are yourself.

If you are with Tao, you will not make these mistakes.

Those who follow Tao may put out the appearance of a personality, for the convenience of other people and to be left alone, while inside they are constantly erasing all these things. They have glimpsed the source that is Tao, and they are aware of emptiness, and so they have no use for personal identities. To merge with Tao, that is their only objective.

Yourself

 Qi. *Self, personal.* This symbol means "itself" and "inherent."

Tao is inherent in the self.

No matter what happens in life, believe in yourself. Don't give that up for a god. Don't give that up for a master. Don't give that up for a parent. Don't give that up for a spouse. Don't give that up for a child. No matter what, believe in yourself.

Not one of these people can live life in your place. Not one of these people knows you like you know yourself.

No god knows you. No master knows you. No fortune-teller knows you. No one can know you if you don't want to be known. Why? Because the future is not yet made. How can they know what you will do next?

Too many people let others dominate them. For what? For the good of the other only. If you let society dominate you, who wins? Society. If you let your parents dominate you, who benefits? Your parents. If you let a master dominate you, who is empowered? The master. If you let gods dominate you, who is enriched? The gods.

And where does that leave you?

The master says, "Study with me, or be relegated to ignorant sorrow." The gods say, "Worship me, or I will punish you in this life and in lives to come." Tell me, what good are associations built on dirty threats?

Tao does not threaten. Worship it and it will not be augmented. Ignore it and it will not be diminished. Follow it and you will be preserved. Oppose it and you will be destroyed. But if you do choose to follow it, you become independent.

That is liberation.

Touch

 Mo. *To touch, to feel, to rub, to caress.* The lower part of the word shows a hand. The upper part is a phonetic, the word for "hemp."

Our lives cannot be sensed whole. We have to feel our way forward. And what we feel, we have to trust.

One of the hardest things is to trust our own feelings. Beginning with well-meaning parents and teachers, we hear so many instructions that thwart and ridicule our perceptions that we eventually internalize this mistrust of our own feelings. Far too many of us have voices of doubt playing continuously in our minds. Soon, it is hard to feel anything genuine, because these voices are always telling us that we are wrong.

Disappointments and setbacks reinforce these voices. Maybe we start out trying to be extraordinary. "I'll be great!" we vow, but then we stumble a little, and the voices become louder.

But we have to stick to our perceptions and to our feelings. That is where experience, philosophy, and self-refinement come in: we know that we have accomplished things, we know that we can coordinate what we perceive with established principles, and we trust that our beings are finely tuned enough to accurately feel what is around us. What we do in life is up to us and will not be known all at once. Therefore, we have to feel our way along, little by little, building the vision to know what we are individually meant to do. We can't let doubt interfere with our touch. We have to trust our touch.

True

Zhen. *True, real, genuine, superior, simplicity.* The key to this word is in the center, where the rectangular shape enclosing two lines represents an eye. Above and below are parts of a phonetic, a single word divided in two that is derived from a word meaning "point" (as in the point of an arrow). The entire word *zhen* is a borrowed meaning in which the eye looks at something that is pointed out as true.

In the past, people accomplished in Tao were called *Zhen Ren*—True Persons—in part, perhaps, because it was they who pointed out the way.

The paintbrush doesn't make pictures without a hand.
The zither makes no music in its case.
A votive painting cannot stop a bullet.
Place a shuttle in a loom and it cannot weave alone.
Put a key in a lock and it cannot turn by itself.

A plane needs a carpenter.
A book needs a reader.
A field needs a farmer.
A wheel needs a potter.
A boat needs a sailor.
An altar needs a worshiper.

In all these cases, it is the person that makes things true.
Why blame an object for being something it isn't?
That is why, in olden times, one who followed Tao
Was called a True Person.

Material

Cai. *Material*. On the left is the character for "wood." On the right is a phonetic.

You must work with your material in order to do anything with it.

Pieces of timber will not assemble themselves into a building. A block of marble will not carve itself into a statue. A bolt of silk will not weave itself into a garment.

In all these cases, one has to work with one's material. And each material will assert its own nature. Its character must be respected and accommodated during manufacture—those who ignore the character of their material are doomed to failure.

Wood, though cut, is still a living material, expanding and contracting with the seasons, and so a good cabinetmaker allows for wood movement. Marble, though of fine texture, cannot be cut too thin or be left unsupported, and so a good sculptor chooses a subject suitable to expression in stone. Silk, though beautiful, must still be sewn together with its grain properly oriented, so a good tailor aligns the grain correctly to make the garment last.

When we first imagine a project, that is merely a plan, a beginning point. Actual accomplishment depends on our skill and our material. We have to work with our materials, until our hands acquire a knowledge of their own and we can shape things according to our will. These simple principles of craft apply to our lives as well.

Each day, we grow older. Each day, our bodies and minds progress toward thresholds of change as if already scripted. Aging and the way we change according to internal cues form the "material" of our lives. So if you want to work with your material, you need to do something with your life at all times. Work with your material. Touch it, knead it, feel it. Do something and then work with what comes forth. Then true talent, power, and genius will inevitably emerge.

Prisoner

Qiu. *Prisoner, confinement, prison, criminal case.*
A person (the symbol in the center) is placed inside
a square that represents a prison.

The worst imprisonment is the one we impose
on ourselves.

Addiction is most abhorrent to those who follow
Tao because it destroys the health of the individual, corrodes the
mind, and cuts off freedom. How can one follow Tao if one is
hampered by illness, confusion, and immobility? It is not possible.
Therefore, when the most important priority is to follow Tao, the
imprisonment of addiction must be broken.

It doesn't matter what rationalization you might use to justify
your addiction. It doesn't matter what difficult circumstances
led you to adopt it in the first place. Those who follow Tao seek to
understand any and all their addictions and to destroy them with
great resolution. That takes discipline, of course, and effort. But
there is no other alternative. At the same time, cleansing yourself
of your addictions gives you a wonderful way to work on your
spirituality. You don't need esoteric doctrines. Simply work to free
yourself from your addictions and the rest will be easy.

Those who follow Tao believe that all people are intrinsically
pure. They believe that this purity is obscured by education and
socialization. But they also believe that the far greater barrier to
our original purity are addictions. Strip them away and the true
human will be there.

Vomit

Tu. *To vomit, to spit.* The word for "mouth" is on the left. The word for "earth" is on the right and is a phonetic. One spits or vomits upon the earth.

There is a wise immediacy to vomiting.

As uncomfortable as vomiting is, it can be very instructive. Usually some indiscretion or illness brings us to the point of throwing up, and if we have to throw up, we might as well learn something from it.

There is a certain genius in the quickness of vomiting. Somehow, a body knows when it has to get rid of something offensive. Once it has decided, there is no holding back. Regardless of whether it is socially acceptable, or smart, or a good time for it to happen, the vomit will come. It doesn't matter if we use all our might and all our concentration to try to stop it.

In the throes of whatever brings on such nausea, all other concerns are blocked. It doesn't matter what work you have or where you are. Maybe you don't even hear what someone is saying to you. This is akin to perfect concentration.

And when vomiting happens, it happens mightily. It is forceful and complete. Retching can be so powerful, it will leave your abdomen sore for days. Again, perfect concentration. Perfect action with nothing left undone. Ahh—don't we usually feel so much better after throwing up?

It's astounding how many years we will put up with bad relationships and horrible jobs and stupid social obligations, all because we think we must. It's amazing how we will smoke and drink and eat bad food and stay out too long in the sun, even though we know it's bad; we do it over and over again anyway. Isn't it because we don't let our innate genius take over? If we did, we would not tolerate what is bad for us for even a second. We should take this as a challenge. If we know bad things have come into our lives, we should forcefully expel them as quickly as possible. Without a doubt, we will feel much relieved.

Root

Gen. *Root, origin, base.* On the left is the character for "wood." A phonetic is on the right symbolizing "territory" or "land."

Stubborn wood. The condition for lasting and thriving.

Have you ever had to chop down a tree? The hardest part is getting the stump out.

Have you ever done a bad job weeding? If you don't get the roots, the weeds come back.

Have you ever seen a tree toppled over? Sometimes the roots can still generate new shoots.

Have you ever tried to trace where vines come from? If you don't follow the runners all the way back to the roots, you have not found the whole plant.

Have you ever planted a tree? The most important point is to provide adequately for the root system.

Have you ever watered a plant? Unless the water reaches the root, your efforts are useless.

Therefore, if you want to know strategy, know when and how to destroy the root.

If you want to develop thoroughness, know how to find the root.

If you want to knock something down, go to the root.

If you want something to stand, establish the root.

If you want to know yourself, go to the root.

Deep

Shen. *Deep, profound, ardent, intense, extremely.*
On the left is the symbol for "water." On the right is
a phonetic.

To be deep results from accumulation. To be profound results from great experience.

The young are often brilliant, intense, beautiful,
athletic, innocent, and joyous. But they are seldom profound. Why?
Because to be profound requires a vastness of experience and wisdom that the young seldom possess.

One who is of Tao is profound.

You may want to discuss philosophy with such a person, but it
will be like trying to use an enormous net: you will be entangled in
the countless threads and colors, whereas the sage can pull on one
strand and have the whole come together.

You may seek to know such a person, but it will be like wandering in a huge forest: wherever you turn, there will be a new
trail, each one mysterious to you, but each one well known to the
sage.

You may want to be with such a person, but it will be like
swimming in the ocean: you will wonder how the waves come
continuously and seemingly without pattern, but the sage swims
as effortlessly as a dolphins.

That is how profound one of Tao is. Can you become such a
person? Yes, if you continue to follow Tao. Sometimes it seems futile, until you realize how deep the accumulated years of devotion
have made you. Then you too will see that you are as deep as the
vast oceans.

Talent

Cai. *Talent, power, genius.* This represents the trunk of a tree. Since the trunk is the best part of a tree to use in building, it has come to symbolize the best part of a human being—talent.

It doesn't matter what use a builder has in mind; he or she must use wood according to its properties. In the same way, people should act according to their inner talents.

There was once a young gymnast training for the balance beam. One day, her coach tired of her mistakes. She was unable to achieve the perfection he demanded. When she came down from the beam, he beat her so severely that she died.

When the officials investigated, the other girls admitted that they were routinely slapped and berated. They thought it was the price they had to pay to become famous. When her parents first sent the gymnast to the coach, they knew of his methods. After she was killed, though, they felt great remorse. Is it better to have a daughter who, seeking fame, died at the hand of her coach? Or is it better to have a daughter alive and laughing?

It is part of the method of cultivating Tao to seek perfection. Indeed, in the various schools of Tao, the training is as harsh as what happened to the gymnast. But is this really worth it? Each of us has his or her own level of talent. That level of talent is something we must discover, and a trained eye may well help us uncover it more quickly. We should be training not to achieve some ideal level of accomplishment, but the level that is our own perfection.

Talent, then, is our greatest worth. It is the potential that we must bring out. If the level of that potential doesn't result in world fame, that is quite acceptable. Fulfilling your talent is not a matter of pleasing a coach or parents. It is a matter of doing what you were meant to do.

Eccentric

Guai. *Eccentric, strange, to blame, monster, prodigy, miraculous, astounding, odd, ugly.* On the left is the symbol for "heart." On the right is a phonetic showing a hand above the earth.

All those who follow Tao are eccentric.

All those who follow Tao become eccentric. If you do not want to be that way, then do not follow Tao.

How eccentric? Look at the word *guai:* you will be both strange and miraculous. A monster and a prodigy. Ugly and astounding.

Why will you be this way? Look at the word *guai:* you, unlike others, will plow the field of your heart. You will gain the growth that only the earth of your heart and the light of your mind can produce. You will till that ground over and over again, cultivating it as no one else can do. That ground will change forever.

You will see that growth and you will replant, and you will harvest again and again, and the growth will change and develop in the course of the seasons.

Others will tell you that they do not farm the way you do. You won't care. Others will comment on your choice of what you grow, how you grow it, and when you choose to harvest; they will wonder at what you do at night, and they will voice surprise behind your back at the farmer you are becoming. You won't care. You'll keep going in the mad faith that you know how to plant, that you understand the comings of the sun, the whisperings of the wind, the dance of the waters. Soon, you won't hear the others talking at all. You'll only see your field, hear the breezes, smell your crops, touch what no one else can touch.

You will be strange. You will be ugly. You will be odd. But you will be a person of Tao.

Two

Er. *Two*. Very logically, there are two strokes. But symbolically the word refers to the pairing of heaven and earth, the pairing of yin and yang.

There could not be heaven without earth. There could not be yin without yang. There cannot be perception without comparison. There cannot be comparison without subjectivity.

Oddly enough, no two people will feel the same about Tao, even though they may live next to one another. You may puzzle over this, and you would have every right to. If Tao is the greatest reality, why isn't it the most fundamental "objective" reality there is?

The ancients explained this clearly: Tao is called the One. It is the fundamental reality. The philosophical problem with One is that there is no two—but we always need two in order to perceive anything. Unless we are referring to a special and rarefied state of consciousness, we cannot perceive anything without having the contrast to see it (you cannot, for example, see white on white or black on black). That is why the ancient scriptures say that from One comes two, because there must be duality for there to be existence.

These two are called yin and yang. We need white to know black. We need space to see a line. Everything in life we know because of distinctions.

The trouble comes from the fact that no two people judge things the same, and therefore they do not have the same perceptions. No two people can stand exactly in the same spot in the world. Each one of us approaches the world—and Tao—from our own unique viewpoint. None of us can perceive Tao the way someone else can. We can only perceive Tao the way we can.

We cannot perceive the One, because we can never be standing apart to view the One. That would be a contradiction. It would be One plus ourselves and then that wouldn't be the true One anymore. So everything we feel of the world is always the Tao of two, or to put it another way, the relative Tao. And the relative, by definition, cannot be the absolute One.

Perception

Jue. *To perceive, to feel.* The top half of the word means "to learn" (see p. 43), while the bottom half means "seeing" and also "to awaken."

(see p. 43)

Tao has to be known with the entire self, not through words.

What does one do in the face of the most fundamental flux in existence that is Tao? Well, you could either stand in one place and let it all go through you, or you could take advantage of your volition and try to act within the flux.

Some spiritual systems hold that a deity comes first. Therefore, they encourage obedience over perception—you have to know what the laws are, but you don't have to know why. But the ancients taught a different perception of reality. They felt that the cosmos was great, but impersonal. There was no chance to influence the workings of time and nature according to the wishful thinking of humans. Thus, the methods of Tao are not ones in which one tries to conform with what a Big Mother or Big Father tells people to do. Instead, it studies ways to act wisely within a constantly shifting dynamic.

This makes perception paramount. One needs to become sensitive and experienced in operating within an always developing set of surroundings. What counts then is neither dogma nor obedience to some divine ruler. What counts is perceptive action within the all-encompassing flux of Tao.

Origin

Yuan. *Origin, head, principle, money.* The two horizontal strokes represent what is above, the two vertical strokes represent a person.

The origin is within each of us. To know Tao we must know ourselves.

All initial attempts to feel Tao in life are tentative. We must attune ourselves, and we must come to understand ourselves before we can fully understand Tao. That is all right, because we are originally Tao too, and a full understanding of the self will therefore lead to an understanding of Tao.

Over and over again, the sages in many different cultures advise us to know ourselves if we would want to understand others. All of us are interlocked, and all of us are projections of each other. By the same token, we must know ourselves before we can know the vast and endless Tao.

If you want to be receptive to Tao, you must be active and search personally. Being receptive to Tao doesn't translate to mere waiting. Instead, you must have the receptivity that is an open mind roaming in infinity.

Bone

Gu. *Bone*. The top part represents the head and shoulders, while the bottom is the word for "flesh." Thus, the word shows the bones as support for the body.

Those who follow Tao try to reach what is most fundamental.

Bone is the symbol for what is most fundamental about our bodies. Without it, we could not support ourselves. It is the framework for our movement and our functioning. It protects vulnerable organs. When we die, it is the last thing to decay; bone can last thousands of years longer than flesh can.

It is the endeavor for all those who follow Tao to penetrate to the bones of their lives. The ancients called the superficial "playing with the skin and the hair." We want the deepest, the most basic. We want the bones and marrow.

The ancients spoke of changing one's marrow through spiritual living. That means reaching the deepest parts of yourself in order to cleanse and transform them. Those who do this can never be shaken, because they succeed in securing the absolute core of who they are. When you consider how deep you need to go in the way you live, remember bone.

Withered

Ku. *Withered, dry, decayed.* On the left is a picture of a tree, here representing wood in general. On the right is a phonetic, the word for "ancient" (see p. 19).

That which is old is stiff. That which is young is soft.

That which is old grows stiff and then decays. That which is young is pliant and soft. Therefore, those who follow Tao follow the way of softness in order to avoid death.

There are many ways to apply this ideal. You could interpret it literally and so try to maintain whatever limberness you have. Or you might understand it to mean that to harden your position toward others inevitably leads to your downfall: the dogmatic—the stiff—are often the first to be undermined.

The tree in the word *ku* gives us a hint of how to proceed. A tree, on the inside, is hard but flexible. Without the bone of its interior, the tree could not stand. But neither is it so stiff that it will not give way to wind and storm, and neither is it so stiff that it has no life: on the outer layer, the tree is soft, and there it channels life.

The tree is often used as a metaphor for meditation. It is still, but inside, there is great movement. So too must we understand how to combine hardness and softness. If we do, then we can avoid the withered state.

Old

Lao. *Old.* This is a picture of an old person whose hair has grown long and white.

In the time it takes for one's hair to grow both long and white, how much of life one has survived and experienced?

Yes, we want to talk of personal growth. Yes, we want the freedom that personal growth imparts. But the process of personal growth is so vast, and our time is so limited. Personal growth therefore takes place in the context of our aging. How much skill can we acquire before our fingers tremble and our hair has all gone white?

The ancients were fond of lecturing that there were some things a person wouldn't understand until they were older. That may be. A more accurate statement is that there are different levels of consciousness, depending on one's age. Each one is valid for that age. What a teenager knows is perfect for being a teenager—anyone else looks stupid doing what a teenager does. What an elderly man does is perfect for an elderly man: anyone else doing it engages in absurd mimicry. Each level of consciousness is not only appropriate, but imperative to one's age. Certain types of knowledge are most relevant and true at certain ages.

It take time to learn. And it is important to take the time, to give ourselves the time. If we rush through things, if we don't take the time to properly learn what we should at a certain stage of life, we will arrive at old age having learned nothing.

Enough

 Gou. *Enough, fully.* On the left is a phonetic that is the sign for "shell." The word on the right signifies "no more room." The limits of the shell's interior have been reached—that is enough.

Do everything fully. Then you have done enough.

It's so hard: we try and try, and when we judge our results, we are disappointed. But as long as we have tried fully, as long as we have done our utmost, then there is no reason for sadness.

That's easy to say when we witness a world-class performance by a champion athlete. Or when we hear a famous opera star give a flawless performance. Afterward, they will say modestly to their admirers, "I did my best." Of course, their best was not only ten times better than what any of the rest of us could ever muster, it was good enough to break records.

But none of these people can be you. And none of these people can live your life better than you. That's important to remember. The measure of success is not necessarily how you fare in competition, but how fully you live your life. When the archer pulls his bow, he pulls it fully. He cannot pull any other bow at the same time, and the bow can only bend in the way that it was made to. Neither the archer nor the bow question their function or their nature. They act and focus themselves on the target.

If the archer shoots a bad shot, can he do it over? He cannot. He can only fault himself if he did not pull the bow fully or if his attention wavered. If he hits a bull's-eye, can he save the act? He cannot. It is over, and to try again, he must again pull the bow fully. In the same way, we should only regret when we do not live our lives fully and in a way that is most true to ourselves. If we live our lives as fully as the archer pulling the bow, then we have done enough.

Belly

 Du. *Belly, abdomen.* On the left is the character for "flesh." On the right is the phonetic meaning "earth" (see p. 6).

The belly, our base and center.

How many people think of their bellies? How many people are aware of what goes on there?

Why think that spirituality is a matter of the head? Why think that abstract and academic speculations of philosophers will give you answers?

Our bellies are where we were connected to our mothers.

The bellies of women can give life.

Without the belly, you could not digest food—you'd be capable of precious little philosophy on an empty stomach.

Without the belly, you could not sit up straight.

Without the belly, you could neither twist nor turn.

Why do we ignore the belly? When we are under stress or disappointed, it is often in our bellies that we feel pain. When we are consumed with laughter, we laugh until our bellies hurt. When we are threatened, we instinctively protect our bellies.

Just as the word *du* combines the body and the earth, so too is the belly the true foundation of our efforts.

Fountain

Yuan. *Fountain, spring.* On the left is the character for "water." On the right is the phonetic meaning "source" or "origin," shown as follows: the angle on the top and left represents a cliff, the dot represents the water gushing out, and the vertical lines are the streams running from the spring. This is a modern form of the word; originally, "fountain" and "source" were one word. (See page 250.)

The true source of all spirituality is within you.

We have within us an inexhaustible well of knowledge. Unfortunately, so many of us spend our time distracted with surface matters that we never become aware of the deeper waters.

We have within us a vast world of creativity. It is just that the view is often blocked by our preoccupations.

We have within us the very source that is Tao. However, that source is buried deep within.

It frequently happens that, when establishing a new place to live, a spring has to be dug out. We know it is there by the water that trickles down from the hill and by the plants that are nourished there, but we cannot see it and must clear away brush before we can find it. Springs are frequently found on ridges and mountainsides: when it rains, the hills fill with water, and the springs flow. The water is there; only we must find where it comes out.

With our personalities it is the same. Within each of us is a fountain of knowledge, wisdom, and creativity. It is good to clear our mind each day so that new life and creativity can flow from the fountain. It is good to use our minds each day. If you have a good idea, use it so that you will not only accomplish something, but so that you can make room for new ones to flow into you. It is good to cleanse the mind of distractions and indulgences and to make it clear. When that happens, you have the opportunity for Tao to gush up in you like a fountain.

Part Fourteen

SIMPLIFYING

Retreat

Tui. *To Retreat, to decline.* On the left is the character for "path" or "movement." On the right is a person shown in profile, taking a step backward.
Know when to advance. Know when to retreat.

Countless numbers of the ancients tried their best to improve the world with their teachings. Some wandered incessantly to heal the sick. Others traveled tirelessly to negotiate peace between warring nations. Some taught children and cared for orphans. Others went to the imperial court to preach the wisdom of Tao. Others roamed far and near, championing the weak against oppressive officials and landowners. Some taught the people how to grow their crops better. Others preserved precious books for the generations that followed. But somewhere in each of their lives, the ancients knew when they had done enough. They knew when it was time to simplify.

Some of them left the world in weariness and disappointment: advocating Tao in a world of the avaricious and power-mad was a difficult, perhaps even futile task. More than a few of the ancients were either exiled or persecuted into retreat by small-minded emperors or jealous enemies. Warriors tired of the fighting and yearned for peace. Scholars reached great fame only to be dismayed by the emptiness of it. The ancients understood that the young of every generation would want to test their vigor and idealism against the world. But they also saw over and over again that such struggle would always be limited by the vicissitudes of the world. Thus, the teachings of the ancients incorporated the art of simplification.

When one has seen that ambition and elaboration are no longer necessary, the teachings of Tao are still useful. Some would say that these teachings are even the heart of following Tao. Action in the world is inevitable. But there is a place for quiet too.

It is in the time of simplification that the voice of Tao becomes more audible.

Butterfly

Die. *Butterfly.* On the left is the character for "worm" or "insect"; it is used in all words having to do with insects and reptiles. On the right is the phonetic meaning "leaf " (a combination of the words for "generation" and "wood").

The butterfly is a reminder that life, though ephemeral, is beautiful.

One of the ancients of Tao, Zhuang Zi, wrote a famous parable called The Butterfly Dream. In the dream, Zhuang Zi dreamed he was a butterfly. When he awoke, he asked if he was now a man who had dreamed he was a butterfly or a butterfly dreaming that he was now a man.

In counterpoint to this is another ancient legend about butterflies. The story of the Butterfly Lovers tells of a man and a woman so in love with one another that the gods changed them into butterflies, to be reincarnated for eternity, so they could find each other in love over and over again.

Life is ephemeral.
What we take for reality is puzzling.
Do we want to repeat over and over again
To have dazzling beauty?
Or do we tire of the repetition?

Butterfly, butterfly,
Where do you go?
You are born for a day
With breathtaking beauty.
And you come back over and over again
To perform the same dance of life.

Dream

 Meng. *Dream.* The two cross shapes above the rectangular symbol for "eyes" indicate that the eyes are closed. Below is an enclosing shape, indicating someone curled up asleep. Inside this shape is the sign for "night." One is curled up asleep at night, dreaming.

When we awaken and are able to see clearly, what will it be like?

Life is like a dream, the ancients say, so there is no good in taking it too seriously. What is real one day disappears the next. What seems like a good thing as it approaches suddenly turns into something disastrous instead. Out of nowhere, we receive good fortune. And through no fault of our own, we can attract the enmity of others. It is no wonder that those who followed Tao of old gave up on society. Weary of the betrayals and uncertainties of life, they retreated instead to a life that would more likely reveal what this dream was all about.

Life is strange and unpredictable each day, and to make matters more odd still, it is over all too quickly. Like a dream, fragmented consciousness that it is, there is nothing to which we can cling. But if life is a dream, is someone the dreamer? If life is a dream, does it take its elements from some other reality? If life is a dream, what can we do to wake up?

Stop living your life as if you were investing in a dream. Inquire into who the dreamer is and what the dream portrays. Then you will not be far from Tao.

City

Zheng. *City.* On the left is the character for "earth."
On the right is a phonetic, the word for "success."
It shows a person on a high wall holding a weapon.
When there is success after war, the king returns to
build an even higher wall to defend the city.

Society's accomplishments are symbolized in the
defensiveness and exclusivity of the city wall and the
aggressiveness of a man with a weapon.

It seems that everything is in a city. Government. Culture. Architecture. Services. Entertainment. Society. Family. Excitement.

But the word *zheng* contains an important lesson for those who follow Tao: a city is a place that is built up through conflict; success is symbolized by the triumph of a weapon. Therefore, as great as the old cities are, there are times when one must either temporarily retreat or finally leave. While Tao is everywhere, it is difficult to follow its spiritual path amid the colors and din of the city.

We won't pretend that the ancients never went into the city. But they knew it was something provisional, even dangerous. And for all the complexity of city structures, there were few places where it was rooted in the fundamentals of life.

Nation

Guo. *Nation, country.* The square around the perimeter represents the borders of the country. Inside is the word for "land": the small square is a mouth, representing a person, and the line below multiplies that symbol to mean "all people." On the right is a weapon for defense.

The very idea of a nation is built on exclusion and defense.

The young and ignorant never seem to tire of fighting. A child fights when his toy is taken from him. A youth joins a gang and fights for streets that ultimately never belong to him. A fascist is swayed by doctrines of superiority and attacks foreigners. A rebel is moved by talks of nationalism and works to overturn a government. A racist supports the idea of ethnic cleansing and genocide.

The tragedy of all these attitudes is that they confuse loyalty with chauvinism. As we are growing up, our elders exhort us: be proud of your culture, protect your country, champion the cause of your ideals. When these ideals are expressed with loyalty, the result is often great deeds of heroism and creativity. When these ideals degenerate into chauvinism, the terrible excesses of racism, brutality, and extermination emerge.

One who follows Tao eventually realizes the futility of racial and national divisions. This takes a very long time, because so much of our learning is subtly influenced by these ideas. Indeed, some might say that these social features are rooted in our very emotional makeup. But being a follower of Tao has never been about doing what society says. Being a follower of Tao means walking the spiritual path. And the ideas of race and nationalism cannot be valid on a path that goes through a land with no borders.

Bridge

 Qiao. *Bridge.* On the left is the sign for "wood." On the right is the sign for "lofty." This word was originally derived from a drawing of two pieces of wood stacked on top of each other to form a bridge.

A bridge can span a river, but it cannot span Tao.

A bridge is really one of the marvels of human ingenuity. Not only have some been engineered to span far reaches in places of unstable weather or difficult terrain, but some are also of great beauty. Slender arches, masterful roadways adorned with statues of heroes, simple wooden structures gracefully allowing admiring views of a garden—bridges everywhere have been wonderful structures.

But the attitude that leads us to build bridges cannot necessarily be used to know Tao. We might be tempted to say: "The two shores are yin and yang and Tao is the bridge." With that we have solved all philosophical problems! But that would be mistaken.

Tao cannot be so simplistically grasped. It cannot be neatly accounted for and a solution engineered. Accessibility can only be gained on an individual basis and not en mass. Why? Because accessibility occurs in the mind of the individual. No bridge can span that enormity.

Bridges are a wonderful path to walk on with our feet. But the path of our mind can know no bridges: only leaps.

Fame

 Ming. *Name, fame, reputation.* The square shape at the bottom is the sign for "mouth." At the top is the word for "evening," represented by a picture of the crescent moon. When your name is called morning and night, you are famous.

Those who follow Tao take no name.

Those who follow Tao take no name. They do not seek fame. They do not care about their reputations.

The thoughts of others are traps. Those who follow Tao do not let themselves be defined, bothered, or admired by others.

To live the life of Tao is a lonely life. It is very tempting to wish for fame, support, and admiration. But this is contrary to Tao.

When you find yourself in despair, wishing you had a comfortable life of fame and fortune, take a moment to reflect: that you have this feeling shows that you know what is contrary to Tao. After you have noted this, remember to continue working toward your goals.

Those who follow Tao avoid fame.

Same

Yang. *Same pattern, model, manner.* On the left is the character for "wood"—patterns and models are often made of wood. On the top right is a phonetic, the word for "lamb," and on the bottom right is another phonetic, the word for "eternal" (showing sparkling water flowing unceasingly). This idea of the pattern of water is borrowed to enhance the meaning of *yang*.

When looking at the crowd, why be impressed? When looking to one's own needs, remember the fundamental.

It's very instructive to sit outside a public restroom.

Look at the people going in and out. No matter how beautifully and richly dressed they are, they still have to go.

No matter how many expensive things they carry—shopping bags, portable phones and computers, purses, books, luggage— they all have to put them down before they go about their business.

If everyone has to divest themselves of all their trappings at least a dozen times a day, isn't that a good reminder of what's important? Wealth leaves all too soon. Beautiful clothes have only limited usefulness. And in our private moments, our concerns are all too common.

Therefore, why hanker after the ephemeral? Why try to gain an advantage over others? Why put on airs?

Add

Da. *To add, to pile up.* On the bottom is the symbol for "join" with the sign for "bamboo" above.

Let things be as they are. Don't try to add to them.

People never get tired of being elaborate. If one thing is good, two will be better. If a little brightness is good, then gilding will improve things. When will people learn to stop interfering?

Left to its natural course, life will go along in the right way. People only make things worse when they interfere. When they feel good, they want to feel better. When they are rich, they want to be richer. If they can run a certain speed, then they try to run faster still. It is a rare wisdom that knows how we feel at a certain time is just right. It is a seldom seen sensibility that remains content with the wealth one has. It is an unusual mind that can accept how fast one runs.

Sooner or later, if you try, you will feel Tao. When that happens, just let it come into you on its own. Don't try to make it "better." Don't try to hold on to it. Don't try to add anything to the experience. Tao will come to you and you need do no more than accept it. Remember the hand in the word *da*. It tries to add where nothing more is needed.

Reduce

Jian. *To reduce, to lessen, to diminish, to subtract.* On the left is the sign for "water." On the right is a weapon cutting something smaller. (Compare this word with the interior of "nation" on p. 232. Where the line below the square there represents augmentation, the line is above the square here, signifying diminishment.)

To cut is to lessen. To fling water into drops is to lessen. To reduce is the skill of masters.

Beginning cooks often load many flavors into their cooking. It takes a master chef to put one or two things on a plate and let the quality and flavors of the food speak for themselves.

Beginning flower arrangers often crowd many flowers into dramatic bouquets. It takes a master arranger to dominate a room with a single flower.

Beginning boxers punch and kick, striking many times, but landing few blows. It takes a master boxer to dodge and then topple the opponent with a few moves.

Beginning poets often write long pieces filled with dramatic allusions and metaphors. It takes a master poet to hold an entire world in just a few lines.

Beginning musicians often go for dazzling scales and stunning orchestrations. It takes a master musician to express everything in a simple melody.

Beginning architects often assemble too much ornamentation. It takes a master architect to display only proportion and material.

In the beginning of our efforts, we often do too much. Anxious to be noticed, we decorate whatever we do with great excess. After all, if we don't yet have the sensibility to do exactly what we want, why not dazzle the world with flourishes?

But those who follow Tao are spare in what they do. They seek quality. They know that just the right actions, arranged in just the right way, at the right time is all they need. That takes time to learn. But there is nothing better than to see a master who has reduced his or her art to its finest essence.

Dust

Chen. *Dust, the world.* Below is the character for
"earth." Above, used phonetically and tripled to signify a herd, is the character for "deer" (the horns are
on top, the body in the middle). When the deer run,
dust is raised.

This world is dust.

Poetic descriptions of the world as being like red dust have become so deeply rooted into the language that dust and the world
are synonymous. For centuries, people—spiritual and secular—
have referred to the affairs of the world as so much dust.

Do you place great value on your accomplishments?
The world is dust.
Do you think that you can easily grasp the meaning of life?
The world is dust.
Do you think that the problems of life ever ease?
The world is dust.
Do you want to place all your faith in society and things?
The world is dust.
Do you think yourself to be great?
The world is dust.
Do you feel overjoyed with good news and depressed with
the bad?
The world is dust.
Do you take the slights of others seriously?
The world is dust.
Do you hesitate when you hear of Tao?
The world is dust.
Do you have doubts about when it comes time to leave the
world?
The world is dust.
Do you fear death?
The world is dust.

Obscure

Mi. *Obscure, infatuated, intoxicated, to deceive, to beguile, to enchant, to bewitch.* On the left is the symbol for "path" and "movement." Above is a phonetic, the word for "rice."

To the one of Tao, his or her path is clear. This path, to the outside observer, seems confused.

Those who follow Tao live according to their own experience, not according to the beliefs and dictates of society. They see the movements of the stars and planets. They note the blowing of the wind. They observe the turning of the seasons. They feel the revolving of the earth. They breathe in the freshness of the air. They taste the purity of the waters. They see the movements of the animals and birds. They hear the sounds of the trees. They study the lives of people. They read the patterns on rocks. They remember how dynasties rise and fall. They delight in the pleasures of food and wine. They relish digging in the fields. They cautiously enter into conflict. They champion peace. They meditate on silence. They heal with herbs. They resonate with music. They imagine with painting. They work for achievements. They exercise for agility. They count the innumerable. They acknowledge with modesty. They thrill to the great. They remember death. They celebrate birth. They support their friends. They replenish in solitude. They use their hands. They tread with their feet.

What use do they have for the artifice of society? They purposefully hide themselves. It is not that they intentionally try to mislead. It is just that they would prefer to be left alone.

Common

Su. *Common, vulgar.* On the left is the character for "person." On the right is a phonetic, the character for "valley."

The ambition of one who follows Tao is no more than to know the valley spirit.

Common people are not truly common. Ordinary people are not truly ordinary.

A person of Tao is common. A person of Tao is ordinary. A person of Tao wants only to live in concert with what is perfectly everyday. He or she wants to live in tandem with the weather, the seasons, the sky, the waters, and the earth. A person of Tao need be no more than a *su* person: a person who knows the valley. A person of Tao is like a valley: wide, open, accepting, seeking the lowest level—a person of balance.

To whittle a piece of wood well, to boil water quickly, to cook a good meal, to repair one's house adequately, to row a boat alone, to throw a pot round, to brew tea to the right infusion, to grow crops that feed families, to know animals, to write what one thinks and feels, to walk nimbly, to concentrate completely—all these seem like ordinary things. All a person of Tao asks is to be able to engage in these ordinary things well.

There is honesty in such direct living. Those of the salons might call living close to the land vulgar. Those of Tao merely smile and walk off into the woods. They would rather be vulgar and in touch with Tao than to be at the pinnacle of social refinement and be vulgar to Tao.

False

 Jia. *False, to borrow.* On the left is the character for "person." On the right is a phonetic. The word in the center is meant to indicate a corpse. The two lines attached to it mean misidentification—one line means affirmation, while two lines mean negation. Someone goes to identify a body and sees that it is not the person he feared it was, and so this situation is extrapolated to mean "false."

So much of life is false. When the disguise is finally pulled away, will it be too late?

There was once a scholar who never tired of study. He read until he could barely see; he wrote until his fingers became callused. His devotion to study was great, but he did not attend to any other matters and lived in deep poverty. It took him ten attempts before he passed the examinations and became a high official. By then, his hair was white, and his health was ruined. He attained wealth and fame, but old age and infirmity made them useless.

There was once a youth, handsome, and with skin as soft as a girl's. He never read a book; he never took up a spear. At twenty, he inherited his father's title and wealth. He enjoyed riding a magnificent horse, kept company with gamblers and playboys. He spent his inheritance on wine, and whatever was left he spent on women. All his life, he knew only hunting, gambling, carousing, and the pleasures of courtesans.

Of these two lives, which was more sad? Of these two lives, which was more noble?

Tao and the word *jia* remind us: this body, this life is only something borrowed. When the sages say that life is like dust, they do not mean that life should not be taken seriously. Rather, they only ask that all of us—from scholar to playboy—put aside what is false.

Abandon

Diu. *To abandon, to throw away, to leave behind.*
This word has the symbol for "palm" on the left, and
"hand" on the lower right. The hands are discarding
something.

Once you gain a foothold on the path, do not hesitate to leave your old life behind.

It so happens when one understands Tao that there is a great
awakening. In the aftermath of that awakening, you may understand that parts of your old life no longer serve you.

We have all had bad habits and indiscreet ways of thinking:
poor eating, drug use, overindulgence in wine, excessive love interests, anger, rage, jealousy, greed, cruelty, selfishness, and a thousand other sins. But coming to an understanding of Tao is to realize a wellspring of purity within yourself. When you taste of that
purity there is no comparison between the goodness of the spirit
and the sins of our addictions. It isn't difficult to see which is better, especially when you experience both firsthand.

It still is hard to give up old habits. Try anyway. Throw them
away. If that means you won't associate with certain people anymore, that's all right. If that means you won't get to drink fine
wine anymore, that's all right. If that means that you have to leave
behind very pleasurable activities, that's all right. Turn to Tao.
And the longer you walk Tao, the farther behind your sins will be.

Forget

Wang. *To forget.* Below is the character for "heart" (remember that "heart" and "mind" are synonymous). Above is a phonetic, the character for "hide," "perish," "cease" (the loop represents the hiding place). The mind ceases to act, that is, no longer remembers.

The ambitious try each day to add more and more. Those of Tao each day seek to make themselves less and less.

If you think that following Tao is to mount on dragons and
    cranes,
You would be better off walking.
If you think that following Tao is to compound the elixir of
    immortality,
You should look simply to what you eat.
If you think that following Tao is mere book reading,
You should travel without a book.
If you think that following Tao occurs through debates,
It would be better to keep quiet.
If you think that following Tao lies in wearing elaborate
    costumes,
Then you should sit naked.
If you think that following Tao requires ordination,
Then you should look further.

So many people enter Tao with overly romantic notions. These are only hindrances. The true masters strive constantly to simplify themselves. They do not care for elaborate rituals, they do not care for fancy costumes, and they will not tell you their name, age, sect, or background. They have forgotten all of this. For them, the pursuit of Tao lies not in acquiring more and more, but in making themselves less and less—until they have reached simplicity.

Return

Hui. *To return.* The image of going back is described by an inward spiral like the curling of smoke or the whirling of water.

Innocence is inside us, and we need to go inside to find it.

Those who follow Tao emphasize the concept of returning. They believe that understanding is possible only when we go to the source of things. Moreover, they believe that we are at our most human when we return to our original nature.

That original nature exists in all of us. It is like a seed, deep inside of us. That seed will not be revealed through religious rituals. We cannot go to professionals and have them give it to us. Nor can we expect gods to come down and award it to us. After all, that seed has been there all along, since before we were born. We don't need someone to give to us what we already have. We only need to simplify our lives and reduce ourselves until we come again to that sacred seed.

Our essential nature, our innocent self, is always in us. Everyone has one, and we only need return to it in order to understand it. Just as the spiral eddies toward the center, we proceed from outer to inner to find the ultimate source.

Part Fifteen

UNION

Together

 Tong. *Same, alike, with, together.* At the center is the sign for "mouth." People are speaking in unison. We all want to belong. And we all belong with Tao.

We all want to belong. We all have a desire for union. From the infant who always wants to be with his or her parents to the lover who longs for a mate, from the lonely person who wants a friend to the acetic who wants to be closer to a deity, the desire for union is overwhelming.

Tao is open to all of us. And in one way or another, all our desires for union eventually have as their underlying purpose union with Tao. Only Tao can offer the harmony and understanding that may otherwise be missing from our lives.

The way to this union is through union with the self. There is a core to us, an inner self that is the key to the greater Tao. If, under the influence of daily stress, we forget or fail to be with this inner self, we are at our unhappiest. But if we achieve union with our inner spirit, then we have peace.

To touch this inner self is not always easy, especially when our troubles are distracting. But the habit of meditation can be very useful in bringing us continually back to this basic self. When we can center ourselves, when we can fit the daily self to the spiritual self as easily as the idea of *tong,* then we begin to feel the joy of union.

Bowl

Wan. *Bowl, basin, cup.* Below is a picture of a vessel or dish. The remainder of the word is a phonetic.

The bowl contains all we need to know about Tao.

Looking at a good hand-thrown pottery bowl can show you everything you need to know about Tao.

The bowl is round.

Tao moves in cycles, and its direction is to return.

The bowl is open.

The ultimate nature of Tao is openness, for that is absolute.

The bowl is useful.

The openness of Tao is not negation; its openness is creative.

The bowl has a center.

On a hand-thrown bowl, you'll see the spiral left by the potter's finger. This spiral, when it goes inward, is returning to the source. In the opposite direction, it is the expansion of all the diverse phenomena. If you would want to know the source of all things as well as to gain all answers, follow the spiral back to the source. If you would want to explore all the diversity of Tao, follow the spiral as it expands.

The bowl is elemental.

Clay comes from earth and water. Pottery is made by fire burning wood. Glazes come from metal. The ancients taught that Tao transforms itself through the five elements of earth, water, wood, fire, and metal. The bowl represents all five elements. Thus do we gain insight into how the abstract becomes tangible.

The bowl is rocklike in conduct.

Steady and correct conduct is the right way to follow Tao.

Empty

Kong. *Empty, leisure, the firmament.* The top portion indicates a cave. The character in the center is a phonetic.

In substance is the power of society. In emptiness is the power of Tao.

The ancients characterized all of Tao as emptiness. But their students, used to judging matters by the tangible, were confused. The ancients took their students to a blacksmith and showed them the bellows. Without the bellows, the blacksmith's work was impossible. Yet, what makes the bellows work? For the ancients, it was the space inside the bellows, always opening and closing. In the bellows of the cosmos, the space was that between heaven and earth.

This is why the wise are seldom disturbed by the comings and goings of life. They see it all as the alternating motions of the great bellows. Nothing is lasting, nothing is permanent. There is nothing that is not in flux; there is nothing that is not simply part of the ongoing expansion and contraction of the empty space inside the bellows.

Therefore, one who follows Tao does not cling to one thing and shun others. One who knows Tao accepts all that comes, because ultimately, it will pass and yet Tao will continue to flow. No matter whether what comes is misfortune or fortune, no concern is needed: there is no actual difference between the two.

None

Wu. *Without, none, no, negation.* This is a pure phonetic borrowing from the word for "dance" (see p. 97).

What is not there is just as important as what is there.

Those who follow Tao place just as much importance on what is not there as on what is there.

When drawing, they see negative space as well as positive.

When looking a vessel, they not only see the outside, but the empty inside.

When they need to maintain a fire, they avail themselves of the bellows—and the usefulness of the empty space inside of it.

When they need to seek a path through a crowd, they look for the space available.

When they consider life, they also consider death.

When they consider the great myriad of phenomena, they also consider the absolute void.

For those who follow Tao, emptiness is as critical as fullness.

The intangible is just as valuable as the solid.

Lack can be good fortune, possession can be misfortune.

And the spiritual can exist in nothingness.

Source

Yuan. *Source, origin, natural, original.* The angle on the top and left represents a cliff. The vertical lines are the streams running from the spring.

As the spring wells up from the ground and gives life, so too does Tao well up and give us life.

It is hard to find a spring. For a time, it is easy enough to follow the streams up to the headwaters. But often, the actual spring is very difficult to locate. It may just be a few drops coming out of the earth, hidden under brambles and brush.

Those drops, however, are the origin of the river. No matter how great a river, like the Nile or the Yangzi or the Mississippi or the Ganges, it starts out from just a few drops. It is good to know the greatness of the river. It is also important to know the river's origin.

Around a river, human beings build their civilization. They crowd its banks, interrupt its flow with dams, span its width with bridges, navigate its surface with boats, fish its depths. People are born, live, and die on the river. The course of a river is complex. Its source is uncomplicated.

The same analogy holds true for the study of Tao. We can busy ourselves with all the talk of right conduct and strategy. We can see how Tao so elegantly sets forth its metaphysics. We can think of its grand history and explore its different methods of longevity. But all of these are mere parts of Tao's flow. If you want to know Tao at its most fundamental, go back to the source.

If you do go back to the source of Tao, you will also find the source of all your questions.

Valley

Gu. *Valley.* The angled strokes above represent the two sides of a valley. The square in the center represents the idea of "hollow."

The valley spirit never dies.

The valley is low. Thus, all things flow toward it.

It is receptive. Therefore, fertility increases in it without it "doing" anything.

It is open, making it the ideal place to receive the sun's life-giving light. Therefore it gains all that the heavens have to offer.

The valley accomplishes everything while doing nothing but being low and open.

By maintaining our modesty and by not considering anything beneath us, we can gain everything.

By being receptive, we can avail ourselves of the spiritual wealth available to us.

By being open, we can receive things beyond what we ourselves might imagine.

Shell

Pei. *Shell, precious.* This is a picture of a cowrie shell, compete with the feelers of the animal at the bottom. In ancient times, cowrie shells were used as money.

What is within a shell is its value.

Every shell turns around its interior. Therefore, it is the center that is important.

Many shells are of great beauty. But which is more valuable— the beauty on the outside or the life on the inside of the shell?

The shell is great armor. It protects the sea creature from the attacks of predators. But the shell must have an opening. The creature must breathe, it must eat, it must excrete. No matter how great its armor is, it must have openings. We who would follow Tao can learn from this example. No matter how much we protect ourselves, true life takes place in opening, not closing.

The shell's usefulness lies in its space. After all, it is the shell's hollowness that allows the sea creature to live inside. So too should one who follows Tao seek the spaces in life. These are the channels through which Tao flows and through which you can assert your will.

It is hard to go through life without a shell. But it is good to remember that it is the center and openings that are important. The shell is just a representative of value.

Shadow

 Ying. *Shadow.* On the left is a phonetic showing the sun shining down. On the right are three strokes depicting flowing hair, meaning "ornamentation." The elevated light on the left shining onto the right casts three shadows.

Shadow cannot exist without light and an object. Light cannot be defined without a shadow.

Unless there is light, how can there be shadow?
And unless there is shadow, how can we know the light?
We cannot have darkness without light.
And we cannot notice light without dark.

When we undertake to study shadows,
We must not be deceived by their appearances.
They are always cast from something:
To understand a shadow, understand its source.

Can you be like the legendary sages of old
Who cast no shadows?
Will you do as they did?
Eating so little that you became ether?

Far better is it to return to the source
Which neither illuminates nor obscures,
Which neither projects nor is cast.
Far better is it to return to Tao.

Pipes

 Yo. *Pipes, flute.* This is a picture of pipes of different lengths—like pan pipes—bound together. The three squares represent the mouths of the pipes, the lines below show the bound shafts.

The hollow and the breath combine to make sound.

The great usefulness of Tao lies in its emptiness.
It is the hollowness of the reeds that makes them pipes.
It is the Tao of breath that is the movement of the universe.
The pipes alone cannot make music.

Pipes make music because they are hollow. But hollowness alone is not enough. There has to be a defined length. Once the length of the hollowness is established, the pitch of the pipe is sure. There is no changing it: a pipe remains true to its character.

A flute is the same, but it has supplementary holes. More nothingness—those who follow Tao are delighted! But the nothingness has to be placed exactly if the nature of the flute—derived from its definite length of nothingness—is to be true. In either case, Tao says that there would not be any usefulness to the instruments without the nothingness there.

But who makes use of that nothingness?

If the music was in the pipes, then they would make music even lying on a rock. But they cannot. It is the player who makes the music.

So don't spend your time looking at the instrument. Listen to the player. You will hear breath through nothingness.

How could so little move a person so much?

Soul

Hun. *Soul.* On the left is a phonetic. On the right is a depiction of a demon—a strange head is atop the sign for "person," and the added loop, which usually means "private," is here used to mean "singular."

The soul is invisible. Is it there at all?

Answer quickly. Do you have a soul?

That is the critical question. And you need to look deeply into that question, because the answer will determine your entire attitude toward the spiritual.

It is not good enough to reason through your experiences and use the soul to explain anything beyond the realm of your imagining. That is too lazy. And worse, it won't give you an answer that will satisfy you.

If you say you are the soul, then where is it? If you are it, why is the soul invisible?

If you say that the soul is inside you, then bring it out. You say you cannot? Then by saying that, you have already indicated the soul.

If you say that the soul belongs to you, then you have confused things.

If you say that the soul is immortal, then you have not looked far enough into the situation. The soul may be immortal, but *why* is it immortal? Answer that and you will be very close to profundity.

If you want to know where the soul is, ask yourself who is considering the question.

Seed

 Zhong. *Seed, class, type.* On the left is the sign for growing grain. On the right is the phonetic meaning "heavy." The seed grows on the heavy part of the stalk.

The whole is in the seed.

A whole plant is contained in the seed.
An entire person is contained in an egg.
Every living thing in the world comes from seed.
And every living thing in the world dies and falls to the earth.
Bodies rot, only to feed the earth and release the seed.
That is true rebirth.

Tao is infinite.
It is a seed of unlimited circumference,
With its center any point in boundless eternity.
Tao is a tiny seed,
Containing unlimited universes in its dimensionless center.

The seed is the whole of what we want to know.
The seed is the center.
The seed is the source.
And the source is the whole of Tao.